# Growing Up Bad?
## Black Youth, 'Road' Culture and Badness in an East London Neighbourhood

**Anthony Gunter**

# Contents

# Acknowledgements

This has been a long, eventful but very rewarding journey which began some twenty odd years ago in a decaying post-industrial neighbourhood of Birmingham, when this 'disaffected' (at the time) young black male left school with one solitary CSE grade 1 in English. During the latter part of this journey (the PhD road via detached youth and community work) I was given invaluable support, encouragement and proverbial 'kicks up the arse' by my supervisor Kevin Stenson, and uncompromising advice by my second supervisor Paul Watt. A big thank you also goes to Hanif Barker who held the fort on many an occasion when this senior youth worker was 'doing ethnography'. Also I would like to thank Melanie Johnson for all those free counselling and support sessions during the period of this research, and Paul Leakey for his support and youth work tutelage. A 'shout out' to all the young people who participated in this study and to the youth work staff team at Manor Children and Young People's Resource Centre. Lastly, thanks to all my family and friends for their support, especially Heather and Mali who have had to endure many years of neglect and monotonous PhD and book talk; also a thank you is owed to our princess madame Aiyana who, along with her 'dollies', regularly kept me company (whether I wanted the company or not) by re organising my office as I attempted to finish off this book project.

Dedicated to Joycelynne Carmen McPherson.

# Introduction

## Researching black British youth

Academic and media interest with black (African-Caribbean) British youth, has largely been restricted to the perennial 'problems' posed by young black men, with young black women seemingly invisible. Furthermore, when looking at the many indices of social alienation and discrimination, it is more than likely that young African-Caribbean males will head many of the lists that detail amongst other things: poverty, mental illness, school exclusions, educational under-achievement and criminal conviction rates. For some commentators, poverty and institutionalised racism are still the root causes for their continued social marginalisation. Such arguments are bolstered by the plethora of reports that highlight amongst other things teacher racism in schools (particularly toward African Caribbean young men)[1] and the prevalence of institutionalised racist practices within the Crown Prosecution Service[2] that deny black (African Caribbean) male defendants equal treatment in court. Young black people are also 'known to be over-represented at every stage of the criminal justice system, including figures for youth offending and in the national prison population' (Greater London Authority, 2003: 3). Other writers play down such politically correct interpretations, preferring to place the blame on an urban black male youth culture that is anti-school and obsessed with the violence and hyper-masculinity of the street (see Sewell, 1997). There have also been a number of empirical studies that have romanticised and championed black British youth subcultures, portraying them either as 'deviant' sites of resistance to institutionalised white racism[3] or as the creative driving force behind contemporary popular youth cultures[4].

Ironically, whilst approaching the issue from differing perspectives all the above discourses seemingly buy into populist news-media stereotypes that portray all young black men as belonging to a larger homogenous collective. From my own experiences as a youth work practitioner, I felt that the academy's pre-occupation with either the black youth problem and/or black youth subcultures, resulted in a theoretically narrow research focus overly concerned with the

1 See, Wright, 1985; Mac an Ghail, 1988; Gillborn and Gipps, 1996.
2 See report by Crown Prosecution Service, 2003.
3 See, Pryce, 1979; Cashmore, 1979; Cashmore and Troyna, 1982)
4 See, Hewitt, 1986; Gilroy, 1987a and 1993a; Hebdige, 1987; Jones, 1991.

'spectacular'. Such research down-played the mundane character of black young people's lives in favour of eye-catching activities such as rioting, 'mugging', gun and knife violence, school exclusions and educational under-achievement, music, and fashion. The black young people that I had worked with—whilst having a love of music, sports and fashion—were just as concerned with obtaining formal educational qualifications, a 'good paying' job, and their own home somewhere in suburbia. In short their aspirations were not too dissimilar from their white working-class peers. In addition black young men growing up in such disparate places as Manchester, High Wycombe and London, whilst sharing a commonality of experience, will nonetheless have to contend with many other challenges that are locally specific. Unfortunately, there is a dearth of empirical research that attempts to holistically explore the complexities and differences within contemporary black British youth experience(s). Such studies that are rooted within local neighbourhood settings would provide a counterweight to the perpetual stereotyping of black male youth, either as the perennial criminal 'other' (Keith, 1993) or the 'darling of popular youth sub-culture' (Sewell, 1997: ix).

## Youth, governance and social policy

The academy's interest in the black youth question was part of a much greater and longstanding tradition—undertaken by various governments and charitable and religious organisations—regarding the problematising of certain sections of the British youth population. Poor and working-class young people's position in British society, as well as their actions, attitudes and behaviour have traditionally attracted the attentions of philanthropists, policy makers—and those self appointed guardians of public morality and sobriety. Indeed, the very concept of youth is intimately linked to a plethora and 'history' of moral panics (Cohen, 1972), 'respectable fears' (Pearson, 1983) and stereotypes ranging from child pick pockets in Victorian England, right through to the 1970s, 1980s and 1990s with their itinerant football hooligans, black muggers, teenage Joy Riders and school girl mothers. The perennial youth question therefore becomes a 'metonym for all that that has gone wrong in society' (Roche and Tucker, 1997: 3) and further allows each generation an opportunity to wax and wane about the ill-effects of modernisation and affluence, which have led to the erosion of traditional values based around morality and duty to the family and wider community.

Some commentators (see Jeffs and Smith, 1987; Jeffs and Smith, 1988; Smith, 1988) perceive youth oriented social welfare policies—from the late nineteenth century to the present day—as an attempt by the state to placate and nullify the potential threats posed by poor and working-class young people, and in so doing maintaining the existing social, political and economic order as envisaged by key members of the bourgeoisie. Indeed, the beginnings of the modern youth service came about through the passing of the 1870 Education Act and the gradual introduction of welfare legislation which transformed youth work into a 'means of producing subjectivity. In return for an opportunity for some amusement, young people would have to submit themselves to improvement' (Smith, 1988: 11). The recent history of the youth service suggests that it is a facility that both local and national governments have shamelessly and expediently used in order to be seen (by the media and the public) to be addressing the 'latest' moral panic of the day. Other commentators, who similarly view British social welfare policy from a neo-Marxist perspective, maintain that youth policy initiatives introduced in the 1970s and 1980s sought to minimise the potential for major civil unrest (Mungham, 1982) amidst record levels of youth unemployment. These policies also highlighted the desire (on the part of central government) to provide a better trained workforce (Williamson, 1993) through the introduction of various youth training schemes aimed specifically at working-class school leavers. Similar state interventions within such areas as housing, social security, youth justice and crime prevention have during the past thirty years or so (Coles, 1995) become even more concerned with discipline and regulation, as witnessed by the introduction of ever more authoritarian policies which have marginalised significant numbers of poor and vulnerable young people by 'systematically removing their access to state assistance, public space and employment' (Muncie, 2004: 208).

There are a number of academics that take issue with the structural determinist influenced arguments concerning the development of youth oriented British social welfare policy. Rather than viewing the state as a coherent and ruthless machine that consciously acts to maintain bourgeoisie capitalist hegemony over its docile masses, there is an opposing discourse which attempts to 'better understand' the complexities of youth policy both historically and presently, through the utilisation of the 'broader notion of [governmentality] and the governmental strategy of sovereignty' (Stenson and Factor, 1995: 176). This approach, which draws heavily upon the work of Foucalt (1977), has enabled social scientists an insight into the way in which the numerous government agencies involved in social welfare are embroiled in the regulation of everyday social life. Instead of viewing power as state centred (which happens to be over bearing and all encroaching), governmentality pushes the theme of the interrelated-ness of social structure, power, knowledge and government at a distance, whereby the state realises how individuals, wider civil society and markets 'have their own logics and densities, their own intrinsic mechanisms of self regulation' (Rose, 1993: 289).

Whereas neo-Marxist influenced writers argue that social welfare policies aimed at working-class young people are mainly concerned with preparing (or training) them for a life of poverty, disadvantage, dead end jobs, and the dole:

> the strategies involved in the government of youth can be viewed as aspects of [governmentality]. This refers to the targeting of the population as an object of government at both the collective and individual levels, in order to foster health, wealth, economic efficiency and social stability.
> (Stenson and Factor, 1995: 174)

Meanwhile sovereignty, through the use of disciplinary practices—such as police surveillance, stop and search, public curfews and other disciplinarian or repressive means of patrolling the borders of youth and other ascribed risk identities (Ericson and Haggerty, 1999)—and training, education and surveillance resolves to enable young people to gain new productive skills and a growing sense of citizenship which enable them to better adapt to the modern day expectations of the global capitalist economy (Rose and Miller, 1992; Donald, 1992). Consequently, instead of viewing governmentality as a specific technique Stenson and Factor, (1995: 174) argue that it:

> constitutes a broad ethos or framework of government, within which discipline [the attempt to produce docile, well regulated individuals] and the sovereign control over territory ... are transformed, realigned and supplemented by new techniques.      (see also, Stenson, 2000)

Stenson (1998 and 1999) further develops the notion of self-governance particularly in relation to the study of young people, and argues that it is important to recognise the interactions between formal and informal sites of governance. Within this perspective, young people's peer group networks, hang-out spots and wider subcultural influences become informal sites of self-governance, in contrast to public modes of government. It is necessary therefore to undertake ethnographic research with young people in order to better understand the way in which they attempt to self-govern their own lives by resisting the official strategies and schemes of governments, policy makers and other statutory and voluntary organisations concerned with disaffected and marginalised youth.

## Youth—Transitions and social exclusion

Coles (1995) identifies three main transition lines or 'careers'—the school-to-work transition, domestic or family transition and lastly the housing transition—that young people must successfully pass through on their way from dependent status (childhood) through to independent status or adulthood. Each of the three 'careers' are interrelated and interdependent on each other. Furthermore they contain 'structures of opportunities for young people' which are themselves 'determined by social and economic conditions' (Coles, 1995: 10) as well as by government policy. During the post Second World War boom years characterised by full employment, the school-to-work transition was seemingly secure and straightforward, with the majority of young people leaving school and obtaining paid employment. As wage earners these young people were also much more likely to make further successful domestic and housing career choices, taking advantage of the prevailing opportunity structures and leaving the familial home of origin to start their own family and/or live independently. By the mid 1970s, however, the social and economic position of many young people within society had become decidedly more perilous due to a world wide economic recession coupled with a restructuring of the labour market. The Conservative Government's social security reforms in the mid-1980s, further compounded young people's increasing marginalisation by raising the age for unemployment benefit claimants from sixteen to eighteen (Coles, 1995).

The collapse in the youth labour market, when combined with neo-liberal government social and economic policies radically altered the structures of opportunities available to young people[5]. By the early 1980s the transitional life stage of youth had become more prolonged, more uncertain and—particularly for those vulnerable groups of young people already disadvantaged by race/ethnicity, class, disability and demographic location—more risky also. A number of working-class young people have been able to temporarily put off having to face the grim reality of unemployment, and have taken advantage of the new educational opportunities afforded to them by the widening participation

5   See, Ashton et al., 1990; Banks et al., 1992; Coles, 1995; MacDonald et al., 1997; Maguire and Maguire, 1997; Roberts, 1997.

agendas of the various colleges of both Further and Higher Education (Ainley, 1994). Nevertheless:

> a significant minority of young people are left out of this process of increased educational participation. Their early 'career trajectories'—now largely absent of employment—lead them progressively towards the edges of their local labour markets.                    (MacDonald, 1997: 169)

Such socially excluded young people who are 'not in employment, education or participating on work-based training programmes' (Not in Employment Education or Training [NEET])—between the ages of sixteen and eighteen—are throughout the course of their lives also more likely to face higher than average rates of unemployment, under-employment, ill-health, poverty, imprisonment, homelessness and limited intergenerational mobility.[6] In response to the growing concerns about the long term risks posed to civil society by an increasing number of disengaged young people, the Social Exclusion Unit was commissioned by:

> the Prime Minister [Tony Blair] to work with other departments to assess how many 16-18 year-olds are not in education, work or training, analyse the reasons why, and produce proposals to reduce the numbers significantly.                    (Social Exclusion Unit, 1999: 2)

New Labour Government policy with regard to young people largely arose from the main conclusions of the Social Exclusion Unit's '*Bridging the Gap*' report (1999), which found that every year, at any one time, nearly 161,000 young people aged between 16 and 18 (or 9 per cent of the age group) were neither participating in formal education or training nor did they manage to obtain any kind of paid employment. Those young people from black and minority ethnic backgrounds (particularly those of African-Caribbean, Bangladeshi and Pakistani origin) were more likely to experience lengthier spells out of learning and work in comparison to their white and Indian peers. Whilst there is an acknowledgement by policy makers and academics about the particular difficulties faced by black and minority ethnic young people both educationally and in relation to a shifting youth labour market, there has been very little (if

---

6    See Blundell et al., 1999; Bryson et al., 2000; Coles et al., 2002; Ermisch and Francesconi, 2001; Flood-Page et al., 2000; Riley and Young, 2000; Social Exclusion Unit, 1999.

any at all) locally situated empirical research with these groups. Consequently, the policy agendas of the New Labour Government have largely been informed by those research studies and theoretical discourses centred on the transitions of socially excluded white working-class young people[7], and has not allowed for a perspective—cross referenced with ethnicity, gender, class and spatial locality—which highlights the specific challenges (both economic and cultural) faced by black and minority ethnic youth.

## This study

Underpinning much of this book is a concern with the range of transitions and post-16 experiences, choices and opportunities (or lack of them) available to young people, amidst changing global and local labour market conditions (see also Ball et al., 2004). Whilst there has been very little empirical research exploring the transitions of black and minority ethnic young people, there is a large body of academic literature devoted to the educational underachievement of African-Caribbean youth, particularly males. As there has been very little attention paid to their life experiences outside of the compulsory education system, it is this gap that I believe this study will attempt to fill. Significantly, this study takes as its starting point Tony Sewell's (1997) school-based ethnographic study 'Black masculinities and schooling' which examines the role that youth subcultures play in the total experiences of African-Caribbean young men's schooling (see chapter one for further discussion).

Whilst acknowledging the importance of subculture within the lives of black young people, this study is nonetheless rooted within a broadly political economic theoretical framework. The majority of studies undertaken within the youth-as-transitions research tradition have been with white working-class young people, and largely undertaken in neighbourhoods and regions of the United Kingdom that have suffered high and persistent levels of structural unemployment (see, Banks et al., 1992; MacDonald et al., 1997, Johnston et al., 2000; MacDonald and Marsh, 2005). These studies have largely been concerned with examining the impact of changing government policies, de-industrialisation and economic restructuring upon disadvantaged young peoples lives. This book is similarly interested in exploring the effects of recent political and socio-economic transformations on young people's lives—particularly black young people who are more likely to suffer lengthier spells out of learning and work (Social Exclusion Unit, 1999). However, the key research question running throughout

---

7    See, Banks et al., 1992; MacDonald et al., 1997

the course of this study is 'how young people from the same locale and from [apparently] the same socio-economic background' (MacDonald et al., 2001: 5) but different ethnicities—black, white and mixed parentage—self-govern their own lives via the influence of the local subculture(s), as illustrated by their vastly divergent mainstream and alternative career paths.

This book seeks to avoid a solely economistic interpretation of the young people's lives. One of the main criticisms levelled at the youth transitions approach is its pre-occupation with the availability (or lack) of waged labour which is perceived to be the 'ultimate goal' for all young working-class (particularly young male) youth. Some critics have argued that this:

> consequent emphasis on production has led to a limited research paradigm focused on 'transition' as a rite of passage between developmental stages of psychological maturity and immaturity, complemented by a sociological transition narrowly restricted to [vocational] maturity and [nuclear] family formation.
>
> (Cohen and Ainley, 2000: 80)

This economist approach explores working-class young people's transitions and mainstream and alternative career paths largely within the context of their increasing social, political, and economic marginalisation. The local and regional settings of much of the youth-as-transitions research might be described as 'socially excluded' areas that traditionally were reliant upon a few key industries, which have since almost entirely disappeared. In the past such locales provided working-class young males—on leaving secondary school—with a ready supply of entry level manual jobs thus smoothing their transitional journey into adulthood. As a consequence of economic re-structuring these same localities now provide limited work opportunities for school-leavers, which in addition to the consequent high levels of youth unemployment, also serves to block many young people's traditional progression route to adult status. Although largely sympathetic to the youth transitions approach and its emphasis on political economic analyses, this book is nevertheless critical of the economistic and structurally determinist bias inherent within this model of youth research. This book gives greater recognition to young people as active human agents (Giddens, 1991) and also draws on the work of theorists and researchers from the academic sub-disciplines of cultural studies and the sociology of race relations; who highlight the importance and impact of micro cultural factors—racial/ethnic identities, music, fashion and peer group networks—upon young people's post-16 choices and experiences (see particularly Nayak, 2003). Significantly, this book highlights the complex interplay between social class, spatial locality, race/ethnicity, gender and spatial locality and their combined impact on the young people's lives.

## Organisation of book

The ensuing chapters of this study will flesh out the above themes. Chapter one, sets out to review the various research studies, news-media/populist discourses, and other literature pertaining to firstly; the perennial black 'youth problem' which has loomed large throughout the entire period of post Second World War black settlement in Britain. Secondly, the black British youth experience(s) as viewed through the lens of contemporary subcultural theory with its concern with questions around identity, hybridity and urban multi-culture. Chapter 2, '*Black East London*', provides an historical overview of the main social, political, and economic developments that have shaped East London, particularly those major changes that have occurred within the past thirty to forty years. Central to this discussion will be the location and exploration of what I refer to as 'Black East London', which is defined and determined by significant levels of black settlement. This chapter will also discuss the extent to which the social deprivation and social exclusion faced by East London's black and minority ethnic and refugee residents is also shared by their white working-class neighbours.

In chapter three, '*Researching youth in Manor,* ' I move on to discuss the key methodological issues, dilemmas and concerns around my research with the young people. The first part of the chapter details my previous history (and familiarity) with the research site, as well as many of the young people who consequently feature in this study.

Chapter four, '*Education, employment and training*', will firstly examine the young people's views and opinions concerning their experiences of secondary school, particularly their relationships with their teachers. I will then move onto discuss the informants post-16 choices, opportunities and experiences particularly with regard further education, paid part-time and full-time employment, as well as alternative employment opportunities 'working on road' doing 'badness'. In chapter five, *Families and home-life*, I explore and discuss the family and home-life experiences of those black young people—as well as many of their white and mixed parentage peers—who are featured throughout this study. A further key feature of this chapter will be to explore black young men's school-to-work transitions, taking into consideration the influence of family/home-life as a counterpoint to 'road culture'. Chapter six, *'Road cultures I*, attempts to both document and analyse the role of road culture in the lives of those young people featured in this study. It is particularly interested in exploring the means by which my informants 'kill time' with their friends, derive camaraderie, joy, entertainment and a sense of identity and belonging. This chapter also assesses the influence of 'badness' and 'rude boy' affectations upon the majority of young people's attitudes, values, 'road postures' and dress codes. Chapter seven, *Road cultures II*, is more concerned with exploring the role and significance of 'badness' within East London Road cultures. Firstly, I look at issues of safety and danger in Manor and other 'places' taking into account the young people's kinship, family and friendship networks. The second part of this chapter focuses upon the young people's perceptions of and experiences of 'badness', and then moves on to look at a small minority of mainly black young men who opt for alternative pre-16 and post-16 career paths centred on 'badness'.

**Chapter One**

# Regurgitating the cool (or threatening?) pose: The 'problem' with black British youth

The stereotyping and problematisation of black youth throughout the history of post Second World War black settlement in Britain, is consistent with the various discourses—both political and policy oriented—that have been framed around New Commonwealth immigration and race relations. Much of the debate around black immigration and race relations has been informed by 'common-sense racist ideologies (Lawrence, 1982). These common-sense racist ideologies draw on the colonialist discourse with its dependence on the concept of 'fixity' as the sign of the 'other' as a representation of racial, cultural, and historical as well as physical difference. Fixity:

> connotes rigidity and an unchanging order as well as disorder, degeneracy and daemonic repetition. Likewise the stereotype ... is a form of knowledge and identification that vacillates between what is ... already known, and something that must be anxiously repeated.
>
> (Bhabha, 1994: 66)

Consequently, the stereotyped portrayal of the African man as the oversexed, physical and bestial 'other' within the colonialist discourse needs no evidence, and can never really be proved. When the descendants of these Africans then begin to settle in Britain, their 'otherness' is soon perceived—within the populist discourse—as presenting a serious threat to the internal fabric of the nation.

During the 1950s and 1960s as more and more non-white immigrants began settling in Britain, one begins to see the racialisation of British politics. Peter Fryer (1984) illustrates this by arguing that both Labour and Tory politicians—fearful of losing political ground, as well as votes to each other— progressively sought to pander to populist forms of racist discourse. There was soon a continuum of opinion which viewed black immigration—from zero tolerance to set quotas—in Britain as the main threat to good 'race relations'. Soon the 'legislators made one surrender after another. Step by step, racism was institutionalised, legitimised, and nationalised' (Fryer, 1984: 381). This new politics of racialisation was characterised by the implementation of a number of immigration acts between 1962 and 1973, which effectively relegated every non-white settler from the status of immigrant to that of second-class citizen. The media driven populist forms of racist discourse were fuelled by moral panics and real concerns about firstly: housing issues, with concern expressed about housing shortages; slum black landlords; overcrowding and the subsequent decay of urban areas; and secondly, as the majority of New Commonwealth settlers tended to be male, there was great concern about sexuality and miscegenation, with lurid newspaper reports about black pimps living off the immoral earnings of white women, as well as those detailing the high incidence of venereal diseases amongst West Indian and Asian men (Gilroy, 1987a).

By the late sixties the discourse on immigration and race relations, according to Paul Gilroy (1987a), moved away from issues pertaining to the increasing quantity of black and other New Commonwealth settlers, to those of culture and identity. The internal fabric of Britain was now seen to be threatened by 'race' differences transmitted through culture and reproduced through the institutions of the family and the education system. The problem with black settlement was then linked to the cultures of its people, specifically with black family life. As a result of common-sense racist ideologies, the black family was perceived as pathological, because of its matriarchal structure as opposed to the patriarchal 'hegemonic family' structure as favoured by the white British bourgeoisie. Consequently, linkages were made between the inadequate black family and the cultures of deprivation and crime that consume black youth in the inner city, as well as the dislocated and rootless 'bastardised' black culture that underpinned it all.

Sheila Patterson's (1965) study of West Indians in Brixton is indicative of much of the subsequent research exploring black family life (Pryce, 1979; Cashmore, 1979; Cashmore and Troyna, 1982). Patterson viewed the black child-mother relationship as dangerously weak with the children seeming to spend more time on the streets with friends than with their mother—who invariably had less time and energy to devote to them. Also she argued that:

> the father-child bond is tenuous, uncertain, or even totally lacking in all but a small minority of working-class-class family groupings. Even in this minority, stabilisation and legalisation of the union do not necessarily occur during the children's most formative years. In consequence, they are often witnesses of the strains and tensions between their parents ... They may also have to adjust to more than one or more step-fathers in

their biological father's place. Once grown up, the male child of such a family is unlikely to feel parental responsibility for his own children, since he has learned early that children are 'women's business.'

(Patterson, 1965: 296/297)

Even at this early stage of non-white settlement, black youth are already being problematised and stigmatised as coming from a culture that is deviant and at odds with the white 'norm.'

The ideological and policy discussions about the 'problems' posed by black British youth in the 1960s, 1970s and 1980s was 'intimately linked to the broader context of the racialisation of British politics and the growth of problem-centred images of the black population' (Solomos, 1988: 86). During the late 1960s and early 1970s the political debate and social policy initiatives in relation to young blacks were based on their perceived alienation from society and its institutions, as a result of them being trapped in a cycle of unemployment, homelessness and cultural/generational conflict with their parents. Consequently, there were fears about the increasing amount of violence in urban areas by young blacks, and their subsequent potential for instigating 'race riots' similar to those being experienced in America at the time. By the mid 1970s the dangers posed by black youth in the inner city was harnessed by the phenomenon of 'mugging' (or street robbery), whilst the urban disorders of the early 1980s further compounded the way in which they were represented in terms of social policy and in the public discourse (Hall, et al., 1978; Solomos, 1988; Keith, 1993).

Black youth in the 1990s fared little better, as concern—both in the public and political arenas—was being expressed about their continued marginalisation and exclusion from many of the institutions of British society. Indeed, it was during the summer of 1995, that the then Commissioner of the Metropolitan Police, Sir Paul Condon, caused outrage and uproar within certain sections of the black[1] communities, when he claimed in a leaked letter that eighty per cent of street robberies in London are committed by young black males in their teens and early twenties. Sir Paul then went on to say in a subsequent letter sent to forty 'community leaders' and MP's, that many of the young black men who were carrying out the muggings had in fact been excluded from school or were unemployed (*Guardian*, 7 July, 1995). In the space of a few days, Sir Paul had managed to replay the perennial stereotype of 'black youth in crisis', playing on

---

1   The tern 'black' as referred to throughout this paper is concerned with those individuals and/or groups of African-Caribbean descent..

the old moral panics of black criminality, black youth unemployment as well as the underachievement—and now disproportionate school exclusion rates—of black school pupils. Black youth as deviant social problem again featured in the headlines of the national media during the winter of 1998, after the broadcast of a documentary on Channel Four, which was an 'exposé of gang rape of black girls by black boys' (*Observer*, 22 November, 1998). The above television 'exposeé', thus added the infamous old stereotype of rampant black male hyper-sexuality to the heady brew of black criminality, unemployment and underachievement.

The common-sense racist ideologies used to frame the various representations of the black family (and its youth) is comparable to the representations of 'dangerous' youth (see earlier introductory discussion), as also constructed in the public and political discourse, with young people frequently presented as actively 'deviant' or passively 'at risk', and sometimes as both simultaneously' (Griffin, 1997: 18). When one then adds 'race' to the history of respectable fears about young people (Pearson, 1983), the framing of black youth as 'problem' within ideological and public debate seems a natural outcome. Black youth as a social problem was further compounded by the intervention of the sociology of 'race relations' and 'ethnicity studies' which rather than challenge many of the common-sense racist stereotypes held about black people, instead sought to theorise them (Lawrence, 1982). Consequently, the early studies of the black settler in Britain tended to pathologise black cultural and social life, portraying a community riven with cultural doubt, that was rootless, weak, dysfunctional and criminally inclined.

## Research on black youth: Pathology and black masculinities

As noted above the sociology of 'race relations' and 'ethnicity studies' tended to pathologise the black communities, with the consequence that black youth as a social 'problem' was now being given academic legitimacy. Furthermore, a great deal of the research concerning black youth by the late 1960s and 1970s was being determined by the public and policy discourses on immigration and race relations, which were concerned with how best to integrate the black immigrants and their children into the British 'way of life'. The notion of 'second generation blacks' as a problem was taken as fact with various research studies beginning to explore the institutional experiences of black British youth with regard to education, employment as well as their position in society at large. Much of the research played up to the 'good race relations' policy oriented discourses, which were concerned with the questions of how best to stop the increasing marginalisation of black youth from the major institutions of British society. There was a growing perception that young blacks were not doing very well in school, that they were more likely to face high levels of unemployment and as a consequence they were taking up deviant lifestyles on the streets—putting them in greater conflict with the police. The pathologisation of black youth as portrayed through research is best illustrated by Pryce (1979), Cashmore (1979), and Cashmore and Troyna (1982), who replay the common-sense racist ideologies of the dysfunctional black family with its intergenerational conflict and cultural confusion, and portray black youth as being caught up in a cycle of deprivation and who are pre-disposed to a life of crime, or confrontation with the institutions of white British society.

The bulk of research into black youth has mainly been concerned with the problems posed by young black men, with debates around young black women being virtually non-existent[2]. A great deal of the policy oriented discourses as well as the various 'race relations' and 'ethnicity studies' borrows from the largely American influenced 'black masculinity studies' best articulated by writers such as Staples (1982), and Liebow (1967). Here the social and historical determinants of slavery and racism are seen as resulting in black masculinities being placed within a subordinate position to those of the white 'hegemonic' masculinities (Connell, 1987). The black male is perceived to be a frustrated patriarch unable to fully enjoy the same degree of power, control and authority as exercised by his white counterparts, due to the emasculating social, and psychological effects of slavery and racism. It is believed that black men have bought into the value system as presented by the white hegemonic model of masculinity, yet there is a frustration on their part due to the effects of institutional racism, as well as the economic decline of the inner city which has restricted their opportunities in the spheres of education, employment and politics. Consequently, black men seek out new ways in which to assert their masculinity by creating sub-cultures that are nihilistic, aggressive, and overly concerned with acts and attitudes which display physical toughness, power, and control, resulting in the oppression of their women and children as well as each other.

Within much of the 'race relations' and 'ethnicity studies' research of black British male youth (see particularly Pryce, 1979; Cashmore, 1979; Cashmore and Troyna, 1982; Sewell, 1997) the peer group is all important, acting as a safe haven away from the hostilities and indignities of the wider white racist society, a

2  Notable recent contributions regarding research with young black women has been Mirza's Young, Female and Black, (1992) and Wulff's ethnographic study of 'Inter-racial friendship' in a South London neighbourhood (1995a).

place to be affirmed and valued. Yet even within the sphere of youth sub-cultural theory, where the peer group represents the site of resistance to the dominant culture by the marginalised group, the black peer group—doubly disadvantaged by their race and class position—is according to Alexander (2000: 386), seen more as a 'cathartic expression of frustrated power and social maladjustment than of positive action and control'.

Even amongst black academics and activists there is a common-sense notion that many of the 'problems' associated with black youth is as a result of a dearth of black male 'role' models or 'elders' in the community, as was the case in:

> traditional African societies ... with young people being entrusted to their elders, heads of craft associations, societies or extended family members for personal development, job training and general guidance.
>
> (Majors et al., 2000: 386)

This state of affairs is attributable to the effects of institutional racism resulting in many young black men wrongly turning to the subculture of the peer group. Academics like Majors argue that this situation can only be rectified by establishing mentoring education programmes[3] to provide constructive interventions into the lives of black young men, particularly during those critical and key transitional periods.

The above discourses on black masculinities and corresponding studies of black urban life assume that all black men are a homogenised collective, tormented by their failure to live up to the ideals of 'white supremacist capitalist patriarchy'. Hooks (1992: 89) asserts that the above scholarship on black urban life—which is also the framework for the academy's discourses on black masculinities—have erased 'the realities of black men who have diverse understandings of masculinity ... and puts in place of this lived complexity a flat, one-dimensional representation'. It further assumes that all black men have bought into the 'capitalist patriarchic' model of wanting to conform to gender role norms, ignoring the fact that there have always been black men ready and willing to construct alternative roles. This 'essentialisation' of the black male subject draws on imperialist common-sense racist discourses that constructed him as the bestial and/or physical 'other'. They are further enhanced by the public and media stereotypes of black men which further play on the 'colonial fantasy', as there are a fixed and

---

3   There have been numerous mentoring projects set up around Britain like those in Dalston, Hackney East London and in Manchester amongst others.

limited set of roles in which the black man can be seen to excel in, and many of these 'constantly repeat and reinscribe *idées fixes*—ideological fictions and psychic fixations—concerning the nature of black male sexuality' (Mercer and Julien, 1988: 145). One such public stereotype is that of the natural black male athlete equipped with a perfectly honed muscular body, mythically combining power, agility, grace and machine like sporting efficiency. It is an arena in which the black man can excel, inviting the envy, awe and respect of his white male counterparts. Even within those sporting areas where black male athletes have overachieved—football, boxing and athletics—they are still overwhelmingly under-represented in the areas of coaching, management, and administration as a result of whites' stereotyped views of blacks physical attributes. Here the sporting success of black sportsmen and women:

> has frequently been explained in terms of genetic superiority and a range of assumed physical attributes, including agility, speed, strength, and reflexes, but excluding stamina, courage, and intellectual abilities.
>
> (Polley, 1998: 153)

The black male body might be eulogised in the sporting arena, but within the social arena it is vilified, caricatured as a powerful and dangerous machine, the physical manifestation of the violent and dangerous threat that is black 'macho'. Attempting to add a new dimension to studies of black masculinities, Majors (1989 and 1990) acknowledges that institutional racism does not result in all black men developing self-destructive and antisocial behavioural patterns. Many black men cope with their bitterness, failures, frustrations and social marginalisation by focusing their creativity into the construction of unique 'expressive, and conspicuous styles of demeanour, speech, gesture, clothing, hairstyle, walk, stance, and handshake' (Majors, 1990: 111). These expressive behaviours are a particular manifestation of what Majors refers to as the 'cool pose' (1989), allowing the black male to show the world that he is a real 'man' regardless of the obstacles placed in front of him. The 'cool pose' does add much to the various discourses on black masculinities, nevertheless it still assumes that black men are a collective who have happily bought into the values of white bourgeois capitalist patriarchy.

## Black perspectives: Theorising race/ethnicity, gender and culture

The political representation of the black male subject as a homogenised 'macho' collective within race relations theory—and as also propagated by certain black male activists and critics—was by the late 1980s challenged by black cultural theorists and feminists, who began to discuss the coexistence of race and physical identification, arguing that it is not realistically possible to reduce issues of gender, class and race to a single 'dominant-deviant paradigm' (Marriott, 1996). Correspondingly, there is a need within black masculinity studies to re-evaluate the sexual cultures of black men (Mercer and Julien, 1988; Mercer, 1993) outside of the narrow stereotypes as determined by common-sense racist public discourses. This new paradigm within black cultural studies places culture—the site for the political and social *construction* of identities as fixed transcultural or transcendental categories—at the vanguard of the challenge to essentialist and fixed notions of identity around race, gender, sexuality, nation and class, signifying according to Hall, 'the end of the innocent notion of the essential black subject' (Hall, 1992: 254). The de-'essentialisation' of the black subject was predicated as a result of the marginalisation of the black experience within mainstream British culture:

> not fortuitously occurring at the margins, but placed, positioned at the margins, as the consequence of a set of quite specific political and cultural practices which regulated, governed and 'normalised' the representational and discursive spaces of English society. These formed the conditions of existence of a cultural politics designed to challenge, resist and where possible, to transform the dominant regimes of representation—first in music and style, later in literary, visual and cinematic forms.
>
> (ibid.: 252)

In addition to concerns over the invisibility and the marginalisation of the black experience, were those theorists troubled by its simplistic and stereotypical character. This led to a significant shift in black cultural politics, a shift that according to Stuart Hall, is best thought of 'in terms of a change from a struggle over the relations of representation to a politics of representation itself' (ibid.: 253).

Hooks (1991; 1992) challenges both 'pathological' and 'patriarchal' interpretations of black family life, arguing that despite the prevalence of single parent female-headed households in society at large, when these households are black there is an immediate assumption that black men have failed in their roles as economic providers. This assumes that economic necessity should be the sole determinant as to why black men and women should create households together. Stansfield (1993) also notes that with regard to empirical research into black community life in the U.S.A.—as in the issue of female-headed households—there is a failure on the part of mainstream scholars to use subsequent findings to explain 'Eurocentric realities'. During the last few decades Stansfield II, argues that increasing numbers of professional white women have taken the decision to have children out of wedlock, and are experiencing divorce in record numbers, subsequently academics are now willing to discuss alternative family structures. Yet he similarly notes that when these same alternative family structures are attributable to the poor or black people, they are re-labelled deviant or pathological. It is important then that research exploring black family life, documents healthy productive households that do not conform to the white patriarchal model of the nuclear family, and thus end the 'erroneous assumption that any household that deviates from the accepted pattern is destructive' (Hooks, 1991: 77).

Within the British context writers like Gilroy (1987a; 1993a) have sought to comprehend the cultural dynamics of agency and race, 'considering how blacks define and represent themselves in a complex combination of negotiations and resistances' (1987a: 155). Black cultural formation draws on the politics and cultures of the black diaspora/Atlantic[4], resulting in the creation of new definitions of blackness, spatially set within the British context, resulting in the reinvention of their own ethnicity. Black expressive culture—with black male youth at its epicentre—is here seen at the vanguard of British 'street' culture as a whole, with black identity viewed as a dynamic, positive and creative force, as opposed to the natural linkage of black identity with that of a 'pathology' born out of racial subjugation and/or social structural constraints. Barnor Hesse (1993) in attempting to rethink the cultural politics of black settlement, argues that the contours of black settlement within Britain are more than residential, rather they are also cultures of movement. As such the:

heterographies of settlement, which narrativise the spatial and temporal institution of the community, appropriate regional Britain both in

---

4   The black Atlantic here refers to those imagined (Anderson, 1991) black diasporic communities within the UK, North America and the English Speaking Caribbean (see particularly Gilroy, 1993a)

iconographic and cartographic vernaculars: Handsworth (Birmingham), Brixton (London), Moss Side (Manchester), Chapel-town (Leeds), Liverpool 8 signify not merely the dispersed incidence of Black Settlement but the traces of agency, assertion, harassment, local politics, recreational routes and cultural expressivity.                    (ibid.: 177)

For Hesse (ibid.) the regionalism of Black identity as well as the geography of Black settlement within Britain—and the black presence within the diaspora—allows for the expression of that identity, defines its politics and re-articulates Britain.

Black cultural theory whilst re-defining the role of black expressive cultures and the black diaspora, tended to concern itself mainly with deconstructing/re-interpreting cultural and political representations of race, ethnicity, sexuality and gender within both mainstream and black popular culture. There was no attempt on the part of the black cultural theorists (Gilroy, 1987a and 1993a; Hall, 1988/1992; 1990 and 1991; and Hooks, 1991 and 1992), either in Britain or America, to use qualitative research methods that might develop a 'grounded analyses of the complex and subtle ways'

(Carrington, 1998: 276) in which 'de-essentialised' black subjects might make sense of their daily lived experiences and social interactions. By reinstating the role and significance of black expressive cultures, which allowed for more realistic portrayals of black life, black cultural theory made no attempt to empirically document how—at both an individual and local level—these expressive cultures are created and communicated, or to explore their role with regard to forming black diasporic identities.

### The ethnographic turn

Claire Alexander (1996) and Les Back (1996) although influenced by the discourses of black cultural theory—particularly agency, race/ethnicity, gender and black cultural formation/hybridity—fall more within the post war British cultural studies qualitative research tradition, as they both adopt ethnographic research methods to explore the real life experiences of black and white British youth. Alexander's ethnographic study of black British youth (1996), takes its cue not only from black cultural theory but seeks to examine the creation of black British youth identities at a micro level, where she is concerned with its form and content as it is lived in the everyday experience. Alexander admits that she is not concerned with macro-structural analysis, rather she emphasises agency and employs the de-essentialised notion of 'culture'. In her usage, culture is dynamic, innovative and creative and resists imposed definitions of 'blackness'.

A further aim of Alexander's study is to move away from 'wide ranging quantitative generalisations', in order to portray a clearer perspective of the black British experience, one which reflects more accurately the qualitative aspects of black life. Her study illustrates how the social and leisure choices of black youth, provide significant insights into the articulation of self-image as well as the creation of individual identities in relation to notions of 'blackness' and the wider society. Whilst acknowledging the effects of racism which place certain limitations upon the movement and choice amongst the available social and leisure options of black youth:

> the individual is able to select leisure options in accordance with the life style and image he wishes to reflect at any given time ... The correlation of social images with lifestyle was most clearly reflected by Frank, who favoured the more upmarket wine bars in the West End and tended to avoid both black venues and the less salubrious white clubs.
>
> (Alexander, 1996: 123)

For Frank 'black clubs had the wrong image, which was defined against the upward mobility and image of success reflected by the wine bars he frequented' (Ibid: 124).

Les Back's ethnographic study (1996) of black and white youth also seeks to comprehend the cultural dynamics of race by exploring issues of belonging, identity and racism, and examines the impact of black youth subculture on white youth and urban multi-cultures. Most relevant to my own research is Back's exploration of the life experiences of young black men and women, particularly where he identifies two variants of racism as experienced by his black informants—'institutional' and 'popular':

> Black young people clearly articulated that it is in the institutions of education and the police that racism is mostly encountered. It is not claimed that these institutions are monolithically racist. However, the racism that exists in these contexts introduces divisions that are being undermined by the cultural alliances being developed within the neighbourhood.                                    (Back, 1996: 168)

The black young people in the study are very much aware of their own unequal life chances in comparison to their white peers.

The more 'popular' expression of racism is the type that young black people might experience on the streets as they go about their day-to-day business. This 'popular' variant of racism draws upon common sense racist stereotypes of black people and are also affected by gender:

> Many of the young men refer to instances in South London where white (adult) people with whom they come into contact 'hold on to their bags tightly' or 'put their heads down and walk away'.     (Back, 1996: 164)

Here—as with Alexander's study—Back is not concerned with a macro structural approach but is interested in exploring the lives of individual young people at a micro level, examining the power dynamics of inter group rivalries and tensions as pre-determined by the social and political relations of gender, class, ethnicity and race.

Whilst Back and Alexander can be said to operate within the parameters of Cultural Studies, Tony Sewell's ethnographic study (1997) falls more within the sub discipline of the sociology of education, where there is a tradition of qualitative research exploring white working-class (Willis, 1977; Corrigan, 1979) and black youths (Wright, 1985; Mac an Ghail, 1988) experiences of school. Nevertheless, Sewell's (1997) work also has local cultural formation as his main focus, exploring how black young men through the sub-culture adopt a range of behavioural responses—what he terms as 'masculinities'—in order to survive and resist the 'white hegemony' of the school. These responses range from the conformists on one extreme of the continuum, right through to the rebels on the other side, whilst the retreatists and innovators held up the middle ground. The majority of Sewell's informants perceived themselves to be conformists (forty-one per cent), 'and their defining characteristic in terms of social identity was an opposition to community and the embracing of [individualism]' (Sewell, 1997: 79).

The next largest grouping in Sewell's study were the innovators (thirty-five per cent). This category of African Caribbean young men accepted the values of schooling whilst rejecting the means. Parental influence was very strong with regard to their pro-educational stance. The most interesting aspect around the black masculinities identified by Sewell is the role played by the more 'negative' aspects of the sub-culture, especially its influence on the rebels. The rebels were identified as core group of African Caribbean young men who rejected 'outright' the values of school, replacing it with the alternative lifestyle of the Ragga influenced sub-culture. Where the ethnic signals from 'some boys, namely the rebels, offers a destructive way of thinking. Its only logic is the offensive language of misogyny, homophobia or hyper-heterosexuality' (Sewell, 1997: 12). Within the oppressive environment of the school the negative aspect of the sub-culture also forces all of the young black men into either the conformist ('Uncle Tom') or rebel ('rude boy') role. As both the teachers and the peer group police these two extreme masculinities forcing the students into an either/or confrontation, where they feel compelled to accept 'essentialist' and 'fixed' notions of black masculinity.

Alexander (1996) and Back (1996) both make significant contributions to the field of Cultural Studies, and more significantly they add an important empirically grounded micro (both local and individual) perspective to the discourses of black cultural theory (Gilroy, 1987a and 1993a; Hall, 1988/1992; 1990 and 1991; Hooks, 1991 and 1992). Yet it is precisely because of both writers' concern with agency, identity, cultural formation and hybridity, that I believe their work to be limited. This pre-occupation with popular culture, whether it be mainstream or at the margins (or indeed both, as is the case with black popular culture) fails to take account of the entirety of their subjects' lived experiences. Whilst it is true that previous research into black life tended to be overly concerned with macro-structural analyses, it can be argued that perhaps black cultural theory—and contemporary cultural studies as a whole (McGuigan, 1992; Murdock, 1993; Garnham, 1998)—has gone too far in the opposite direction. Many cultural theorists concerned with race/ethnicity took issue with those writers working within the sub discipline of the sociology of 'race relations', particularly 'those who have sought to reduce race to the inherent effects of various structures—relations of production, and markets' (Gilroy, 1987a: 16). However, whilst highlighting the limitations inherent within economistic and macro-structural approaches to race/ethnicity and racism, contemporary cultural studies (notable exception here is Nayak's 2003 critical ethnographic youth study) down-plays the importance of the political economy—preferring to theorise about agency, identity, hybridity, and 'new racisms'.

As noted earlier in this book, there have been a number of contemporary American-based empirical youth studies[4] that have addressed the specific difficulties faced by African-American and/or Latino youth growing up in poor neighbourhoods. These studies managed to holistically explore their young informants' lives by integrating micro cultural concerns—incorporating identity, agency, racism, and street subcultural formation, alongside family and peer group relationships—with broader political economy analysis. As such, the post-school career paths of African American and Latino young men was explored within the context of their family/home-life experiences, peer group relationships (particularly the influence of street based youth subculture), schooling, as well as the condition of the local youth labour market. The British youth-as-transition research tradition (see particularly, Willis 1977; Banks et al., 1992; MacDonald et al., 1997), moved away from producing theoretically driven studies about youth subcultural 'style' and 'resistance,' towards empirically grounded, political economic, and policy oriented accounts of young (white working-class males) people's school-to-work transitions. These studies have tended to be pre-occupied with exploring young people's post-16 career paths, within the context of restrictive local youth labour markets, and soaring unemployment levels. However, whilst documenting the 'changing structural situation of young people' (MacDonald et al., 2001: 2)—particularly their fractured and elongated post-16 transitions—such research has particularly failed to adequately incorporate micro cultural analyses of race/ethnicity, racism(s), and the impact of fashion, music, and speech styles.

4   See, Williams and Kornblum, 1985; Macleod, 1987; Anderson, 1990; Bourgoise, 1995

Chapter Two

# Black East London: The nearest far away place

Much of the writing and research about East London has, first: documented the key political, economic and industrial changes that have beset the area over the last one hudred and twenty years; and, second: it has detailed the social and demographic changes that have taken place in East London, particularly focusing upon white indigenous working-class communities and the white ethnic immigrant groupings that have settled in the area. Recent research has centred on the economic and social transformation of the area, exploring the acute economic polarisation and ensuing racial conflict within Dockland neighbourhoods like the Isle of Dogs (Back et al., 1999; Cohen, 1996; Foster, 1999). Although there has been some attention paid to the Bengali community in Tower Hamlets (Eade, 1989; Ali-Asghar, 1996; Dench et al., 2006)—as well as the beginnings of a discussion on the experiences of refugees and asylum seekers in Newham (Bloch, 1996)—there has been very little documented about the lives of East London's large black (African/African Caribbean) and Asian (Indian sub-continent) communities.

## 'Black' East London? Where's it at then?

Where does East London begin and where does it end? The response to this question can come in a variety of forms and permeations, and can be said to be very much dependent upon who is answering the question. Much of what has been written about East London over the years has been influenced by the subjective interests—family/ethnic connections or political motivations—of the writers concerned. Consequently, what has constituted the demarcated boundary of the East End of London has tended to be contested. According to Dick Hobbs:

> The resulting demarcation disputes reveal much about the motivation of certain individuals who, in acquiring the necessary clout to put their views into print, reveal little more than subjective criteria in their choice of subject—matter and focal points of analysis.            (1988: 84)

In the latter part of the nineteenth century political reformers and philanthropists like Charles Booth (1889 and 1902) were documenting the impact of industrialisation upon the exploited urban poor in East London. For Booth, the East End centred on the areas around Whitechapel, Stepney, Poplar, Limehouse, Shoreditch and Bethnal Green. Yet by the early 1900s Sir Walter Besant (1901) was re-defining the East London boundary in order to take account of the influence of the docks in attracting workers and housing developments in the hitherto suburban districts of East and West Ham.

By the 1950s East London had again been transformed from the unique area as described by Booth (1889 and 1902) and Besant (1901), through modern industrialisation (development of gas, dock, railway and manufacturing industries) and popular democracy. Yet, the various studies of Young and Wilmott (1957) and Wilmott (1966) on East London and carried out by the Institute of Community Studies were, in the main, still subjectively centred on the old familiar East End of Bethnal Green. Indeed, as was the case with those writers (Bermant, 1975; Fishman, 1979; White, 1980) concerned with those older East End Jewish communities, and is still the case today with those commentators on the area's Bangladeshi communities (Eade, 1989; Ali-Asghar, 1996) who might probably also define East London in terms of Whitechapel, Stepney and Bethnal Green. Hobbs (1988) for his study, subjectively defines East London as the 'one-class city' whose boundaries are not set by any physical sign posts like roads, buildings or boroughs, rather:

> the East End has evolved as an exclusively working-class society ... a disparate community bonded by a culture rather than by any single institution or governmental agency. This one-class society locates its own boundaries in terms of subjective class definition, and east of the City of London you are either an East-Ender, a middle-class interloper, or you can afford to move sufficiently Far East to join the middle-classes of suburban Essex.                                    (Hobbs, 1988: 87)

Hobbs' East London encompasses the boroughs of Tower Hamlets, Newham and Hackney; but only up to Stamford Hill, where he argues North London culture permeates. This demarcation includes the buffer zones of Waltham Forest, Redbridge, and Barking and Dagenham, where the two classes reside 'if not in harmony, then in the same borough'.

Michael Rustin and co-contributors (1996) to *Rising in the East*, the multidisciplinary volume exploring contemporary East London, view the area as being chiefly made up of the six London boroughs of Hackney, Tower Hamlets, Newham, Barking, Dagenham, Redbridge and Havering. With the boundary line marking the beginning of the east falling 'more or less where it always did, at Aldgate' (1996: 2). The boundary lines for Rustin's (1996) and Hobbs' (1988) East London, are artificial:

> as neither the inner city nor the suburbs confine themselves neatly within these political boundaries. Nevertheless, East London … is a distinctive region. It has had, over two centuries, a concentration of the poor, of newcomers and immigrants, often from overseas, and of polluting industries which were unwelcome in more privileged districts. It has been widely regarded as a source of social problems and dangers, and has attracted its reformers and missionaries because of that reputation.
>
> (Rustin, 1996: 2)

Vikki Rix (1997) goes further than both Hobbs (1988) and Rustin's (1996) boundary demarcations, by referring to the London East sub-region which includes the inner London boroughs of Hackney, Tower Hamlets, Southwark and Lewisham and goes right out into the suburban localities of Dartford, Thurrock and Havering.

On my part, whilst accepting and acknowledging both Hobbs' (1988) and Rustin's (1996) definitions of East London, my own subjective demarcation of East London is to distinguish it in terms of significant black (African/African-Caribbean) settlement. East London unlike areas of South, North and North West London is not renowned for its black communities, yet there is a significant pattern of black settlement within the neighbouring boroughs of Hackney, Newham, Waltham Forest and—although to a much lesser extent—Tower Hamlets. According to the 2001 census, the spatial location of the black communities[1] within these four East London boroughs tends to be concentrated within certain wards. Interestingly these wards—within Tower Hamlets, Hackney, Newham and Waltham Forest—are all clustered together and overlap borough boundaries

---

1 The 2001 census describes these black communities as comprising of as black Caribbeans, black Africans or black 'others'.

## Post-war black settlement

East London has always been a place of refuge for those fleeing religious or political persecution, as was the case with both the earlier Huguenot and Jewish settlers to the area. Currently, East London is still receiving large numbers of new migrants from all over the world—including those from Eastern Europe, Somalia, Democratic Republic of Congo, Kurdistan, Sri Lanka, Nigeria, Afghanistan and Iraq—some of whom are asylum seekers and refugees. Particularly over the past two decades Newham had received a large number of refugees and asylum seekers (see Bloch, 1996), however, the number of people being supported by the Local Authority has fallen dramatically. In 2008 there was a 66.5 per cent drop in the number of refugees and asylum seekers in Newham compared to the previous year (Newham Council, 2008). This drop came about as a result of refugees and asylum seekers no longer being eligible for support from individual local authorities, instead they are required to seek support through the National Asylum Support Service administered by the Home Office.

East London contains three of the most ethnically diverse local authorities in the Britain. Newham's Black Asian and Minority Ethnic population (London Borough of Newham 2007) stood at 64.6 per cent; Hackney's non-white ethnic groups comprised 60.4 per cent of its total population, whilst Tower Hamlets non-white ethnic population stood at 48.6 per cent (2001 Census).

The black presence in London is not a late twentieth century phenomenon; indeed there were reports of African soldiers in the city stretching back to the Roman times. There has been a continuous black presence in London since at least the mid sixteenth century (Faizi, 1986) particularly as a direct consequence of the trans Atlantic trade in African slaves. Indeed by 1700, there were estimated to be 15,000 blacks living in London, rising to 20,000 by 1787 (Commission for Racial Equality, 1996).

The beginning of post Second World War New Commonwealth immigration to Britain was famously heralded with the arrival of the Empire Windrush to Tilbury docks in 1948, with amongst its cargo over 400 West Indians[2]. Yet it was not until the late 1950s that significant numbers of blacks, predominantly from the Caribbean—with Asians from the Indian sub-continent arriving soon after—began to settle in East London. During this early part of the post war period, East London was not the first port of call for African-Caribbeans, initially

2   See Mike and Trevor Philips (1998) detailed and vivid account on the impact of the Empire Windrush in 1948.

they tended to settle in West (Notting Hill) and South (Brixton) London. When those West Indians first arrived in 1948 they were put up in Clapham Common deep shelters before finally moving on to either Brixton or Notting Hill. This was to set the pattern of West Indian settlement for the foreseeable future.

Even before the onset of the Second World War, London was losing a large percentage of its population to the suburbs and home counties. The area now covered by Newham (formerly West Ham and East Ham) in 1921 had a population that peaked at 444,000 whereas by 1949 this figure had declined to 296,000 (London Borough of Newham, 1999). The major reasons for this migration was as a result of the decay and degeneration of many inner city areas. Many of these areas were also notorious for crime, prostitution and bad housing conditions. Unfortunately, it was these same areas that the early West Indian migrants found themselves having to reside and settle, as a result of landlords being un-willing to rent to them in other areas and as there was depleted housing stock in London as a whole.

In London the type of employment offered to West Indians was poorly paid—as was the case with their unskilled white counterparts—and tended to be with London Transport, National Health Service, General Post Office, the railways or in the various factories. Those African–Caribbeans that did later on settle in East London would have been attracted to the area because it offered employment and cheap, but poor housing. Heavy industrial and manufacturing employment could be found in the numerous factories (including Ford Motors at Dagenham, ) that grew up around the docks (including large international concerns like ITT, Unilever, and Tate and Lyle), and again in East London there were also opportunities to work in the numerous service industries (NMP/CARF, 1991).

## East London: A history of violent racism

The various ethnic groupings that have settled in East London since the seventeenth century have had to contend with traditional indigenous white working-class hostility and resentment; expressed through the support of extreme right-wing politics and violent racism (Husbands, 1982 and 1983; Fielding, 1981; Newham Monitoring Project, 1991). None of the various immigrant groups that have settled in Britain during the last two hundred years have managed to avoid widespread animosity (Panayi, 1993). Nevertheless, there is a history of white working-class cultural insularity and of hostility to outsiders that makes the East End unique amongst all working class communities in

Britain' (Husbands 1994: 570 and 1982). Racism is part of 'East London's ideological inheritance' (Hobbs, 1988: 11) as illustrated by the long tradition of racially motivated violence against a plethora of ethnic groups. Husbands (1982), charts these traditions back to the seventeenth and eighteenth centuries where there was widespread animosity directed towards the Huguenots. Such territorial defensiveness and ethnic vigilantism helped fuel the politically motivated anti-Jewish disturbances of the late nineteenth and early twentieth centuries. During the inter war years the East End—fuelled by its ideological inheritance—provided a fertile environment for the rapid growth of anti-Semitic extreme right-wing organisations such as the British Union of Fascists.

By the 1970s racial violence and organised fascism became embedded within East London as witnessed by the growing support for the National Front (NF). During this period the NF established an advice centre in Canning Town (Newham) specialising in white housing problems, as well as the first branch of the Young National Front which was based in Barking (Newham Monitoring Project, 1991). East London experienced increasing levels of violent racism in the late 1970s, in Waltham Forest alone there were reportedly seventeen fire bomb attacks on minority ethnic communities between 1979-1981 (*Waltham Forest Guardian*, 20th November 1981; cited in Hesse et al., 1992: 4). Across East London: nine apparently racially motivated murders occurred ... between 1978-81, and in 1985 there were numerous attacks on the homes of Asian families in East London, some of which resulted in the death of the occupants (Bowling, 1998; see also Hesse et al., 1992).

It was within this context of longstanding white working-class East End cultural insularity and hostility toward outsiders, that the British National Party (BNP) was able to mobilise local support in order to record an historic council by-election victory in the Millwall ward on the Isle of Dogs (Tower Hamlets) on 16th September 1993. However, the election of an extreme far-right councillor to an East End Borough Council did not occur in a vacuum, rather, it was the end result of years of political scapegoating of immigrants and ethnic minorities. During the 1970s support for the National Front (NF) in both national and local elections had centred on the inner East End and certain other parts of London and the United Kingdom (Husbands, 1979 and 1982).

There have been a number of empirical studies exploring community life in East London during the last twenty years that have highlighted white working-class hostility towards local black and minority ethnic communities[3].

3 See, Cornwell, 1984; Hobbs, 1988; Cohen, 1996; Foster, 1999; Back et al., 1999; Philipson et al., 1999.

It seems that fundamentally the intrinsic ideological importance of the notion of 'community in present-day East London lies in its opposition to everything that is new and different and to the possibility of change' (Cornwell, 1984: 53). However, the Isle of Dogs is even distinct within the East End itself and is characterised by long-term neglect, which has been exacerbated by the closing of the London Docks. The subsequent regeneration initiatives—like the building of the Canary Wharf tower amidst acute shortages of affordable social housing—of the London Docklands Development Corporation (LDDC), since its inception in 1981, and the developers only served to stir up anger and resentment amongst an increasingly marginalised and fragmented white working-class community on the Isle of Dogs (Foster, 1999). Significantly, this anger was:

> not directed at the at the LDDC or developers—that war had been waged and lost. It was directed at an altogether more vulnerable target: Bengali households, frequently forced to move to council housing on the Island against their will. They became scapegoats for 'local' white people's frustrations. (Foster, 1999: 251)

The BNP was able to feed on the powerlessness, frustrations, local grievances and long standing prejudices of white working-class residents of the Isle of Dogs, in order to further their own political agenda. This unique local political culture was also manipulated by the other mainstream political parties in the area including the Labour party, the Conservatives and principally the Liberal Democrats (Keith, 1995). However, as Husbands (1994) points out, it is important to remember that the Isle of Dogs—as with much of the inner East End of London—has a long history of distinctive anti-ethnic (outsider) politics.

In the May 2006 local elections the BNP became the second largest political party in the outer East London Borough of Barking and Dagenham capturing eleven of the thirteen council seats that it fought. The successes of the Barking and Dagenham BNP campaign was built upon exploiting white working class anxieties over the Borough's acute housing problems and rapidly changing demographics. They falsely claimed that the local council had a secret scheme to give African families £50,000 to buy local houses (*Guardian*, 8th July 2006). However, according to Butler et al. (2008) during the past 20 years Barking and Dagenham's overall ethnic minority population growth has been quite small despite the large despite the large percentage change (according to 2001

Census the Black, Asian and Minority Ethnic population stands at 14 per cent).
Nonetheless:

> What this marks is a massive change for a borough that until the 1990s
> was an almost exclusively white place with the exception of a couple of
> housing estates on its western boundary with Newham ... these 'first time'
> instances are more significant than larger increases in actual numbers in
> boroughs which have lived with heterogeneity longer.
>
> (Butler et al., 2008: 134)

## The docks, modern industrialisation and the local economy

The local economy of East London has traditionally been built around heavy industry, manufacturing, small craft workshops and the docks. Much of the impetus for the economic development of East London as an industrial powerhouse can be traced back to the building of the London Docks in the nineteenth century. Indeed, the borough of Newham grew from a cluster of small villages as the railways expanded and the docks were excavated. This first phase of industrial development in East London largely took place in the second half of the nineteenth century (Poynter, 1996), and was concentrated in areas just east to the city of London, in boroughs—like Newham and Tower Hamlets—which bordered the River Lea and Docklands. Many obnoxious industries and public utilities settled in Newham and Tower Hamlets as they were just beyond the controls of the city of London where there was also an abundance of cheap manual labour. Furthermore, there was a great deal of cheap wasteland available for development allied to a good transport network based around the rail and waterways. Consequently, by the end of the nineteenth century, the riverbank from Limehouse to Blackwall was crowded with factories and warehouses.

The next phase of industrial development largely took place in the 1920s and 1930s around the boroughs of Barking and Dagenham, and Havering in southeast Essex. This period:

> saw the emergence of the automobile industry around the Ford plant at
> Dagenham and the establishment of companies engaged in making new
> electrical and photographic products as well as the expansion of more
> traditional cement, chemicals and printing industries.
>
> (Poynter, 1996: 289)

Meanwhile many traditional industries were also flourishing and expanding in East London, cheap casualised labour was in demand in the mineral and soft drinks factories located in West Ham, flourmills, jam, sugar and sweet factories that sprouted in Silvertown, rag and sweated trade(s) that flourished in Stepney and the three 'Royal' London Docks which between them provided eleven miles of quays. Public utilities like the railways also created a great deal of employment, the Stratford depot of the Great Eastern Railway was East London's largest single employer with over 7,000 workers (Porter, 1994).

The post-war economy of East London continued very much along the same lines as it its pre 1945 state, as a mix of the older traditional industries with those newer ones. Those industries which had flourished in the inter-war years (like car manufacturing) continued to prosper during this period. British based companies, like Fords at Dagenham—benefiting greatly from the decimation of many war-ravaged European industries—witnessed unprecedented growth largely due to surging international demand for British products. By the 1950s Fords at Dagenham was running off nearly one-quarter of a million cars from its production lines each year, and expanding at such a phenomenal rate that toward the end of the 1960s its workforce topped the 30,000 mark (Porter, 1994).

This latter period of post war industrialisation has been described as the social formation of 'Fordism' (Liepitz, 1987; Amin et al., 1994), where cars and other products were mass-produced on assembly lines for mass markets. Here, labour was mechanised, routinised and monotonous with machines taking the place of humans wherever possible to assemble auto components. This revolution in the 'mode of production' gave rise to a 'regime of accumulation' and improving living standards, with the growing welfare state looking to help stabilise both labour and consumer markets. The net effect of this system upon East London was quite transforming, as the area changed 'from a zone predominantly of overcrowding, poverty and social disorganisation, into one of ordered and respectable working-class life' (Rustin, 1996: 4). With the post-war economy booming and showing all the signs of having made a full recovery, it was a period characterised by full employment and rising living standards particularly marking out the 1960s as the decade of the affluent worker where in 'Leyton ... the working-class was now able to afford washing machines, refrigerators, radiograms, TVs and even a new Ford' (Porter: 1994: 421).

Whilst the initial post-war period can be viewed as a period of boom and optimism, the basis of Britain's (and particularly East London's) economic success was built on rather shaky foundations (Porter, 1994). The British economy was heavily indebted to—and intimately linked with—its colonial past; so much so, that with the subsequent break up of the Empire (from 1947 onwards) much of the trade advantages enjoyed by British industries within the world markets also declined. Furthermore, whilst many of the war-ravaged economies in Europe and the Far East had undergone a period of re-structuring and heavy investment in new industries and technologies, Britain had failed to do the same. Britain's failure to come to terms with the changing economic world order—increased competition brought about by greater European integration, the easier movement of goods and capital throughout world markets and the collapse of post-war Fordism—resulted in the disintegration of large sections of her manufacturing industry.

## Industrial decline and economic restructuring:

By the mid 1980s the ravages of de-industrialisation, global economic restructuring and neo-liberal Conservative government policies resulted in the collapse of many key industries within East London. This period was characterised by economic re-structuring and mass unemployment on the one hand and by shrinking subsidies from central government on the other, resulting in huge cut backs in the public sector which helped destroy the post war political consensus about the notion of the 'welfare state' and the 'mixed economy' (Mayer, 1994). Within the world markets Britain's industries were ill-equipped to compete with her more competitive rivals—Japan, Korea, Germany, Italy, France and the U.S.A.—as exports were rapidly declining whilst an unprecedented amount of goods and products were inundating the home markets.

Full employment as a feature of the 1950s and 1960s gave way to the period of mass redundancies and unemployment in the 1980s and 1990s. The groups hardest hit in East London were those unskilled and semi-skilled workers, particularly young people and ethnic minority groups (Rix, 1997). Flour mills and processing plants connected with the docks closed, railway related employment was run down, as was the gas works in Beckton. However, the closure of the London Docks was, in truth, the biggest blow of all. During the 1950s it was estimated that the London Docks employed 50,000 workers, yet by 1981 this figure had haemorrhaged to just over 2,000 (Porter, 1994). Unfortunately, none of the East London boroughs managed to escape the negative impact of global economic restructuring and continuing de-industrialisation, but its effect was 'particularly pronounced in ... Hackney, Tower Hamlets, Newham and Southwark' (Rix, 1997: 118).

The onset of post-industrial global capitalism—whilst precipitating the decline of those traditional modes of industrial production—has nevertheless resulted in the unprecedented growth in the financial and service sectors of those industrialised economies. London's unique historical position as world financial centre—derived in no small measure from its pivotal role as the capital of the British empire—further enabled it to take particular advantage of the new world economic order. On average ninety per cent of East London's (specifically drawing on Office for National Statistics employee jobs 2006 data for the boroughs of Tower Hamlets, Hackney, Newham, Waltham Forest) working population are now employed in the service and public sectors—including distribution, restaurants, banking, finance, IT, education, health and public administration—compared to the national figure of eighty-two per cent. Yet this growth in the service sector (particularly IT, business and finance) has not necessarily trickled down and impacted upon the lives of East London's resident populations, many of whom lack the training and qualifications to obtain higher professional and managerial job positions (see Butler et al., 2008).

Whilst the 'official' unemployment rates across East London had improved somewhat by 2007 (see Table 2.1)—unemployment rates in East London according to the Office for National Statistics (ONS) was still rather high in comparison to unemployment figures for the UK as a whole.

Table 2. 1 Unemployment rates in four East London Boroughs ( Jan. 2007-Dec 2007)

| | |
|---|---|
| Hackney | 11.4% |
| Newham | 11.3% |
| Tower Hamlets | 11.7% |
| Waltham Forest | 7.8% |
| Great Britain | 5.2% |

Source: ONS Official Labour Market Statistics

The unemployment rate for 16-24 year-olds in the United Kingdom was 14.5 per cent as of December 2006, with 16-17 year-olds being particularly hardest hit. In London the proportion of 16 and 17-year-olds who were officially unemployed during stood at 42.9 per cent during this same reporting period (ONS, 2006). Youth unemployment is both a global as well as a national and local phenomenon, and is intimately linked to de-industrialisation and global economic re-structuring. In the past many 15-16 year-olds left school at the minimum school-leaving age, to take up a range of jobs—in either industry or the service sector—that were un-skilled and required little or no qualifications. Unfortunately, during the last three decades the employment opportunities available to young people has declined significantly, resulting 'in a less easily identifiable and distinctive youth labour market' (Maguire and Maguire, 1997: 27). Furthermore, government legislation which raised the age for the claiming of unemployment benefit—from sixteen to eighteen years of age—has clearly only exacerbated the situation, by excluding many young people (both socially and economically) from society at large.

## Social and economic deprivation

According to the *Indices of Deprivation* 2004 (ODPM, 2004), the East London boroughs of Hackney (1), Tower Hamlets (2), and Newham (11) were ranked within the top eleven most deprived local authorities in England, with Barking and Dagenham (21) and Waltham Forest (25) not being too far behind. The Government, in arriving at its results for 2004 measured seven indicators including household income, employment, health deprivation and disability, education skills and training, barriers to housing and services, crime and disorder and the living environment. East London and many of its residents are at risk from social exclusion, or what happens when:

> people or areas suffer from a combination of linked problems such as unemployment, poor skills, low incomes, poor housing, high crime environments, bad health, poverty and family breakdown.
>
> (Social Exclusion Unit, 1998: 69)

Furthermore, the problems associated with social exclusion are said to be self-perpetuating and can result in 'cycles of disadvantage' or deprivation that can go on to blight generation after generation, from young children right through to the elderly. Although the concept of social exclusion is relatively new, it is a term that might easily have been associated with the East End of London, if it had been in use from the early nineteenth century onwards. The area has traditionally been associated with poverty, crime, deviance, ill health and poor housing, and as such has always attracted social reformers, journalists, novelists and philanthropists like Charles Booth (1889, 1902).

As a result of the hardships inherent within much of everyday life, East Londoners have developed their own coping strategies and cultures of resistance, including those centred around deviant and criminal activity or what Dick Hobbs (1988) refers to as 'Wheeling and Dealing' and 'Ducking and Diving'. Much of this also has a historical precedence, as the East End's close proximity and economic dependence upon the Thames afforded its downtrodden residents opportunities to obtain and subsequently buy and sell stolen 'corporate' property. Consequently, 'thieving, and the buying and selling of stolen goods became integral to East End culture', (Hobbs, 1988: 103) where it seemed everybody was 'at it'.

Crime, and social disorder in the East End has traditionally been linked to the area's overcrowded and dilapidated housing stock, even today many of the regeneration initiatives (like those Housing Action Trusts in Waltham Forest and Hackney) are aimed at tackling crime and social exclusion by refurbishing old high-rise 'sink' or problem housing estates, or by demolishing them and replacing them with houses. The East End's dire housing problems (which was mirrored throughout all of London) was further exacerbated by the effects of the Second World War German bombing campaigns. Whilst the movement of East London's population to the suburbs and new satellite towns built on Green Belt land outside of London eased the housing problem slightly, it could not really solve the crisis. Unfortunately, the planners—at the London County Council and at borough level—sought to tackle the London-wide housing situation by undertaking slum clearance, by destroying old traditional communities and replacing them with high-rise or built-up estates. In the space of ten years between 1964 and 1974, no fewer than 384 tower blocks had been erected (Porter, 1994). As a further example as to the extent of the policy of slum clearance, during the post-war period Newham Council had built over 30,000 new dwellings[5] creating huge housing developments like the Kier Hardie estate, which encompasses much of Canning Town and the Western area of Custom House. Unfortunately the:

> Planners' Utopias proved tenants' nightmares, as streets in the sky turned to slums in the sky. High-rise architecture killed traditional street-life, atomised communities and produced disaffection, delinquency and crime. Rebuilding replaced substandard housing with social problems that have proved far more intractable.                    (Porter, 1994: 431)

Hackney, in particular—and to a lesser extent Tower Hamlets and Newham— has suffered more than most from the ill-effects of the Planners' Utopias of the 1950s, 1960s and 1970s, where the Borough's physical landscape is festooned with a myriad of high-rise housing estates, and the inherent problems that

5   London Borough of Newham, Environment Department, *Unitary Development Plan*, 1999..

go with them. Newham[6] also has a serious housing problem ranging from a shortage of affordable housing, an ageing housing stock, homelessness, overcrowding, and over-all poor condition of private rented stock.

## Regeneration

During the last thirty plus years or so, beginning with the London Docklands Development Corporation, there have been a large number of Government backed economic and social regeneration initiatives undertaken in East London based upon the concept of partnership. This notion of partnership recognises the need for central and local government to work together with agencies from both the voluntary and business sectors, in order to more effectively deliver real and meaningful change in the East London Region as a whole. Policies and initiatives aimed at regeneration include (and have included); Hackney 2000, Economic Action Zone, Housing Action Trusts, Education Action Zone, planning-free Enterprise Zone, Stratford Development Partnership, Health Action Zone, City Challenge Companies, and the East Thames Gateway area (which is largely East London), all of which bid for grants/funds from central Government and the European Union as well as seeking investment from the private and business sector. These many and wide ranging regeneration initiatives and partnerships operating in East London incorporate such areas as housing, crime and community safety, education, training, health, employment, business investment, transport, and leisure opportunities.

It is the task of the above regeneration and partnership agencies to 'develop interventions and even strategies to enhance the wealth, income and employment available' (Rustin, 1997: 20) in the East London region. As a result of cut backs in public services (during the last two decades) coupled with the reduced/limited powers of local and regional governments to tax and spend as they see fit, many East London boroughs have had little choice but to enthusiastically opt into the many Government backed small scale regeneration initiatives. On the one hand, there are those who would argue that many of the regeneration initiatives have been successful in cutting across political and sectoral interests to bring about real change. Such initiatives managed to access funds from Europe and central government for the benefit of deprived areas, as highlighted by the:

---

6    All information and source material here relating to the housing situation in Newham, draws on London
     Borough of Newham, Environment Department, *Unitary Development Plan*, 1999.

huge scale of infrastructural development that has been taking place in East London, and which seems to continue. The Docklands redevelopments in the Isle of Dogs and the Royals, London City Airport, the planned Stratford Passenger Terminal, the Docklands Light Railway with its various spurs … DLR crossing to Greenwich and Lewisham, the Jubilee Line Extension from Green Park to Stratford … are major developments by any standard. (Rustin, 1997: 21)

On the other hand, there are those who argue that regeneration and partnership programmes are by their very nature too piecemeal to bring about real change, rather they only serve to camouflage the effects of government cutbacks on frontline services like housing, education, transport, and health. Furthermore, many of these regeneration activities fail to address the needs of black and ethnic minority communities, many of whom still face chronic levels of unemployment. As a result of these and other shortcomings:

Overall, there is a broad view that the regeneration is too short-termist, insufficiently identifies investment assets and opportunities, and sticks rigidly to programmes of small scale spending on an annualised and mechanised basis. … the possible links between social and economic, physical and environmental progress are never fully made. It means that the 'jobless regeneration' has become a norm, where only gentrification and /or migration can affect average area improvements. This is particularly acute in the poor districts of otherwise prosperous cities, such as East London. (Clark, 1997: 59)

Regardless as to the critiques of the multitude of regeneration initiatives in East London, the truth is ever since the introduction of 'metropolitan government in 1888, it has been a guiding principle for those governing London that the East End is in need' (Mann, 2008: 31) of physical, social and economic transformation. The 'Thames Gateway Plan for Sustainable Communities' is the most ambitious and complex regeneration initiative in the United Kingdom, and can be observed as a seamless continuation of 120 years of regeneration practice in East London. The programme covers forty miles of the East Thames Estuary taking in East London Boroughs and district councils in South Essex and North Kent. Because of the sheer size and scale of the project it has resulted in the creation of a myriad of quangos and administrative authorities all charged with a range of often blurred responsibilities and tasked with a vast array of initiatives. The main policy aims of the Thames gateway involves the building of up to half million affordable new homes, new transport infrastructure, the creation of a strong and attractive economy for inward investment, and the development of the Gateway as a sustainable eco-region. Within the 'Thames Gateway Plan' also sits the 2012 Olympics and Paralympic Games and the social, physical and economic regeneration legacy commitment to East London that was central to London's bid for the Games. The development of the Olympic Park in Stratford—it is argued by Legacy Now, the London Development Agency led partnership involving a dizzying array of public sector bodies, local authorities, UK government departments and regeneration quangos—will result in 9,000 new homes, a range of new transport improvements, the creation of one of the largest urban parks in Europe, and the economic transformation of East London's Lower Lea Valley area with the creation of thousands of new jobs (Legacy—www.London2012.com).

Chapter Three

# Researching young people: Reflections and dilemmas

As an undergraduate student I had always supplemented my student grant working firstly as a play leader and later on as a part time youth worker. After graduating I continued working with young people whilst undertaking a postgraduate course in Community and Youth Work. Whilst I was being exposed to new and interesting academic discourses, I was still having to grapple with the realities of practice. I was particularly frustrated by the gaps in research pertaining to black male youth, most of the literature either portrayed them as 'sexy' and creative cultural innovators[1] or as deviant and aggressive individuals beset by social disadvantage and alienation[2] (see chapter two). From my own experiences as a youth work practitioner, I felt that much of the discourses concerning black British young men[3] were too narrowly focused around sub-cultural formation; either as a mode of resistance to white oppression or as the creative engine of popular culture. I felt that these themes down played the mundane character of black young people's lives in favour of the 'spectacular', such as rioting, mugging, music and fashion. And to reflect this, research undertaken with such groups would need to focus on a broader range of their life experiences. It should incorporate kinship networks and home-life dynamics as well as school-to-work transitions, rather than just the usual narrow focus on the (usually negative) role and functions of the black peer group via subcultural formation, and/or black pupil-white teacher relations within the classroom and wider school setting.

Whilst I was disappointed with much of the youth research concerning black British youth, I had nevertheless been greatly impressed, as well as influenced, by a number of contemporary (post-Fordist) American-based ethnographic studies chronicling the lifestyles and life chances of young people—mainly of African-American and/or Latino heritage—'growing up poor' in decaying urban neighbourhoods ravished by economic decline, drugs, poverty and racial/ethnic polarisation[4]. Many of these ethnographies took a holistic perspective with

1   See studies by Gilroy, 1987a and 1993a; Hebdige, 1987; Jones, 1991; Alexander, 1996; Back, 1996.
2   See also studies by Patterson, 1965; Cashmore, 1979; Pryce, 1979; Cashmore and Troyna, 1982; Sewell, 1997.
3   As stated in chapter two, the majority of research concerning black youth has tended to focus on young black males, in comparison there has been very little written about young black women.
4   See, Anderson, 1990; Bourgois, 1995; MacLeod, 1987; Williams and Kornblum, 1985.

regard to their young informants' lives, exploring home life dynamics, street sub-cultural formation and the role of the 'crew' or peer group, as well as school-to-work/street hustling transitions. Whilst there has been a good deal of recent research exploring mainly white working-class British young people's school-to-work transitions—particularly in those regions of the United Kingdom that have experienced high levels of structural unemployment due to the collapse of many key industries[5]—I was not aware of any studies that had explored and tracked (using qualitative research methods) British black and minority ethnic young people's movements from secondary school to the work-place/dole office or career 'on road' doing 'badness' (see chapter four).

## A brief profile of manor

I had worked in East London as a youth worker for a number of years before moving on to run the Manor Area Detached Youth Project, an SRB[6] initiative that was to culminate in the building of a new children and young people's resource centre in the local area. Manor is a pseudonym for a local multi ethnic East London neighbourhood that straddles the two wards Hill View and Manor Side. The Hill View and Manor Side wards both have significant black Caribbean populations, consequently almost one-third of Manor residents can be said to belong to one of the black communities (Census, 2001). According to the Index of Deprivation 2004 (produced by the Office of the Deputy Prime Minister, 2004), Manor is ranked as one of the most deprived neighbourhoods in England. Whilst Manor has a diverse ethnic population and can be described as one of the most deprived districts in England, it does not suffer from the acute economic polarisation and ensuing racial conflict that has beset other East London neighbourhoods (see, Cohen, 1996; Back et al., 1999; Foster, 1999). Manor has a number of high-rise tower block 'sink estates' and a large number of low-rise built up estates made up of local authority and housing association housing stock, that includes maisonettes, three storey apartment blocks and small new-build terraced houses. Households in the Hill View ward are more than twice as likely to be council or Housing Association tenants, than households in other wards throughout the borough (according to data from the local authority). Interspersed amongst the many housing estates are privately owned nineteenth century terraced houses, many of which are let out to students

---

5    See studies by Furlong, 1992; Hollands, 1990; MacDonald et al., 1997; Roberts, 1993; Wallace, 1987; Willis, 1977.
6    SRB is the Single Regeneration Budget—an earlier government funded urban regeneration initiative.

and other transient groups like young working-travellers from Australia, South Africa and migrants from Eastern Europe.

## Meeting the young people

*The Pups*

The first group of young people[7] I made contact with through my detached/street-based youth work in Manor (mainly around the Michaels Estate), was a large informal network of up to twenty mainly black young men aged 10-11. The main players such as Simon Peters, Little Man, Mr. Business, Marcus, Dwayne and Mikey would later on become key informants in this study. Furthermore—after only two or three months of being in the field—I soon began to refer to these particular young men and their friends as the Pups. As it was July and the summer holidays were approaching, I initially consulted the young people about the possible trips and activities that they and their peers might be interested in. By about the second week of July I had managed to put together a summer programme—which I was able to subsidise considerably—full of exceptionally cheap trips, activities and residentials. Not surprisingly, word spread round the neighbourhood (mainly via the Pups) particularly amongst the younger age group that Anthony the new youth worker is offering "'nuff cheap trips, Alton Towers and everything'.

The Pups comprised of a core group of seven young men, with an additional sixteen individuals who were loosely attached to the group. The majority of the group were mainly of African Caribbean descent, although there were members who were of mixed (black and white) parentage or of Indian descent. All of the Pups attended the same local secondary school, Manor Park Boys school. They were aged 14-15 during the twelve months that I was engaged in the field, interviewing or 'hanging about' with the young people as part of this ethnographic study. I would refer to these young men as the Pups because they were renowned throughout the entire neighbourhood for their playfulness and cheekiness, always running about play fighting, 'dissing'[8] the older boys and playing sports—mainly football. On the whole they steered away from trouble, preferring high jinx to 'badness'[9].

---

7   For reasons of confidentiality I have used pseudonyms for all the young people and places featured in this study. See appendix 1 for a full cast list outlining the name (pseudonym), age, ethnicity and gender of all those young people featured in this study.

8   'Dissing' is about 'name calling'/'mickey taking' or 'taking the piss' out of one another.

9   'Badness' refers to a social world characterised by 'spectacular' hyper aggressive/hyper masculine modes of behaviour, usually centring on violent/petty crime and low-level drug dealing.

*The Grafters*

As part of the detached summer programme we (myself and staff team) would
take the younger members on various day trips to such places as Lego Land,
Southend-on-Sea, Chessington World of Adventures, or locally based activities
such as bowling, ice-skating and swimming. Each morning we would pick up the
young people (in the mini bus or coach) from the car park of Michaels Estate
Community and Residents Social Club. At the end of each day /activity we
would then drop off the young people at the same place, or if the activity ended
particularly late then I would drop-off each young person to their home. As I
would be dropping off the younger ones, I would see the older boys hanging
about the Michaels Estate and being 'rowdy'[10]. For a good few weeks I would see
them watching me as I drove past in the mini bus, and after a while I began to
stop the mini bus and make conversation with them. As time went on, whenever
they would see me they would flag me down and jump in the minibus to 'kotch'[11]
for a while or else try and get me to give them a lift down to the local chip shop
or off-licence. The Pups and others in Manor would refer to these older young
men as 'Michaels', in that they were identified through their association with
Michaels Estate. Indeed the older young men identified themselves as 'Michaels',
via their attachment to their home specific territory within Manor. During the
course of this study I came to identify the Michaels crew as the 'Grafters', due
to their commitment to earning a respectable wage through physical manual
labour; what those in East London refer to as 'hard graft' or 'graftin'.

The core group comprised of six young men—one black, one mixed parentage
with the remaining four individuals being of white British heritage—but
including up to ten additional mainly white youths who are tightly attached to
the group. The individual members of the group are aged seventeen to twenty,
and as mentioned earlier, are distinguished by their attitude to employment.
All of the Grafters, save one individual, since leaving school have secured paid
employment as labourers, carpet fitters, forklift vehicle operators, or apprentice
tradesmen. The core individuals of the crew—and some of the key informants
of this study—included Lazy Boy, Sick Boy, Sparky, Tony C and Eddie.

10  'Rowdy' refers to young people being loud and boisterous. On-looking adults might view such rowdy
    groups of young people as threatening and intimidating.
11  'Kotch' is where young people will just sit down with friends and make banter or just take the piss out of
    each other.

## Sweat Shop Girls and Young Moms

During those early days as a detached youth worker in Manor, as well as the Pups and the Grafters, I was also in regular contact with a small group of white young women aged sixteen to seventeen who also lived on the Michaels Estate. Initially these young women (Trish, Jodie, Kay and Minty) used to hang around with the Grafters, but soon tired of their 'childishness' and instead sought out the company of a more mature and 'buff'[12] grouping of young men.

On leaving school Trish, Jodie, Kay and Minty had all found paid employment as machine operators in local factories. They managed to work for a year or two before falling pregnant, at which point they then gave up work to care for their newborn babies. By time when I had began the fieldwork for this study, I had lost all contact with these young women, only managing to see them from time-to-time on the streets. I did however manage to follow their changing life circumstances from a distance through various conversations with the Grafters.

## Safe Crew

I did not the meet any members of the Safe crew until well after the summer holidays had ended. I then managed to make contact with them as a result of my growing relationship with the Grafters. This Safe crew comprised of a small but tight collective of three black young men aged sixteen to eighteen; namely Raymond, Griot and Sweet Boy. Significantly, as with the core members of the Grafters, all of the Safe Crew would become key informants for my research and feature heavily throughout this study.

The Safe crew were loosely attached to the slightly older Michaels crew, as they all lived on, and hung around the same estate. The Safe crew were noted for their mild mannered and easy going natures, yet they were also very streetwise and could mix very easily with those youths who lived for 'badness'. Raymond, Sweet Boy and Griot were not interested in 'graftin' for a living or becoming embroiled in badness, they were all enrolled on full time college courses.

## Arms House Crew

The brand new Manor Children and Young People's Resource Centre began a youth club operating three nights a week. Initially the youth nights were very quiet (although members of the Grafters as well as the Pups would pass from time-to-time to see myself and the rest of the youth work team) apart from a

---

12 Young people in Manor call someone 'buff' if they feel that the said individual is attractive, good looking or sexy..

few young people whom we had never previously worked with before. They were all black young men aged fifteen to nineteen and would come in to the sparsely resourced[13] centre to play the Sony Play Station that one of the youth workers had kindly donated.

Within a few months we were able to identify these young men as being part of the Arms House Crew. Arms House is a notoriously 'rough' part of Manor (at least in the eyes of those individuals who live in the neighbourhood) and comprises a number of high-rise tower blocks and new-build housing estates interspersed amongst nineteenth century terraced housing. Initially the Arms House young men seemed quiet and very approachable and at this point there was a core group of just four young men; Redz, Duke, Makki, and Sam. The main interest for this group was music. They consistently badgered me to purchase a mixer and decks[14] for the youth club, in order that they could practice their dj-ing and mc-ing[15] skills. Duke was the dj of the crew and had decks and a mixer in his house and whilst select members of the crew would go round his house to use his equipment, it was felt it would be more fun to mic and dj at the centre, as it would be more like a 'mini rave'[16] every night where 'everybody could get lively' (see chapter six).

The Arms House Crew had hung about in the small green open space area—where the new Resource facility was subsequently situated—since they were very young children, and remembered filling out questionnaires about the proposed 'new centre' many years previously. When the Resource Centre was being built (and was in effect a building site) the Arms House Crew said that they used to 'bun zoots' (smoke marijuana) in the shell of the building and bring girls down there. To many members of the Arms House Crew, Manor Resource centre was their 'youth club' because they had been waiting most of their childhood for such a facility, and even though they were now much older they still wanted to claim what they believed was rightfully theirs.

As a result of the field research undertaken for this study, I managed to spend a lot more time with the various members of the Arms House Crew in many

13  During the early stages of the youth club opening, there were no resources for the young people to use, i.e. there was no pool or table tennis table available for young people to use. The youth club had to rely on a second hand junior sized pool table.

14  Mixer and decks refer to—two turntables (usually technics) and a pre amp small mixer to control input/ output—the basic set up required for a dj to mix and play records i.e. dj-ing.

15  MC-ing, where the young people (or MC in a rave) rhythmically talk over records in order to get a crowd in a rave 'lively' and 'hyper'.

16  'Raving' is a black British term (derived from Jamaica) that has traditionally been used to refer to going out either to a 'dance' either at a night club, shebeen, or house party to listen to music and dance

different settings. Consequently, I identified the group as being comprised of a main core of five young men, but including up to another eleven individuals (young black males) who were loosely attached to this group; their ages ranged from seventeen to twenty one. Whereas the Grafters crew are defined as a group by their attitude to work, the Arms House Crew renowned for their 'bad boy' actions. As a collective the crew project a tough, confident, and streetwise image and revel in the fact that they are from the 'notorious' Arms House area. The Arms House Crew look to perpetrate 'badness' (see chapter seven) and in particular attempt to police the physical space of their neighbourhood by bullying and intimidating their more vulnerable male peers.

## The Poppettes

The Poppettes are renowned for their love (originally) of pop music, particularly boy bands and had actually formed themselves into an all-girl pop group. I did not make contact with many of the young women who made up the Poppettes until after they began attending the youth club in order to practice their singing and dance routines. The Poppettes are a tight grouping of up to seven young women aged sixteen or seventeen who had previously attended the nearby all-girl Secondary School. The majority of the young women were white—apart from two individuals, one of whom was black-Caribbean and the other had mixed African and Irish parentage—and lived on or nearby the Michaels Estate. Initially a few members of the Poppettes had started 'hanging around' with the Grafters (after the Sweat shop Girls had tired of the Grafters company), but soon also tired of the 'boring' Michaels boys, and instead sought out the exciting 'bad boy' company of the Arms House Crew. The key informants of this group who feature heavily throughout much of this study include Melinda, Ayesha, Maria and Kandy.

## The R'n'B Girls

These girls are a tight core grouping of three African Caribbean young women, and one young woman of mixed White and Asian-Caribbean parentage.[17] They were all aged fourteen when I first made contact with them, again they came to the youth club to practice their dance routines normally to the sounds of contemporary R'n'B music[18]. All of this grouping of young women attended the nearby all-girls secondary school and had a (very) loose attachment to the Pups.

17 There are a further seven young women—all black or Mixed Parentage—who are also attached to the R'n'B girls.
18 Contemporary R'n'B music refers to the popular black urban musical form, which centres on singers as opposed to rappers

Most significantly, they were distinguished by their love of R'n'B and other forms of contemporary black diasporic urban music and culture (see chapter six). The key informants in terms of this study are Darlene, Kanya and Tonya.

## Others

Also featured throughout this study are a number of individuals who have no identifiable group attachments, key informants such as Martin, Will, Tall Boy and Charley.

## Doing ethnographic research

As already stated many of the key informants featured in this study are those young people whom I had worked closely with, as a youth worker during the three years prior to the commencement of the field research. Field work methods entailed observing and interacting with my informants within a variety of settings—youth club, on the streets, in pubs and clubs, home environment, as well on day trips/residentials out of town—and recording the observations, conversations and discussions through the taking of detailed field notes. I also undertook semi-structured tape recorded interviews with a number of young people, and held discussions and informal (non tape-recorded) interviews with a number of adults including parents, school teachers, youth offending team workers, police officers and youth workers.

### Ethnography

Ethnography can be said to be concerned with 'making meaning out of others' processes of meaning making' (McCarthy-Brown, 2001: xi), or simply as the 'art and science of describing a group or culture' (Fetterman, 1998: 1). In truth, ethnography is but one of the many empirical research methodologies available to individuals operating within and across the numerous disciplines that make up the social sciences. Some ethnographic studies rely upon in-depth interviews as a means of gathering detailed life histories and other 'social facts'. Likewise, other projects employ the 'participant observation' method as the principle research tool. As is the case with this particular study, many ethnographers draw on a wide range of information sources including documentary and secondary statistical data analysis, in-depth semi-structured interviews, in addition to 'going out amongst the research subjects' (Armstrong, 1993: 7) to undertake detailed and direct observations. A key principle of ethnography is that detailed explorations of the social world are undertaken within 'natural settings', as opposed to those 'artificial' or imposed environments as to be found with experiments and surveys. This 'naturalist' perspective[19] further maintains that:

> in order to understand people's behaviour we must use an approach that gives us access to the meanings that guide that behaviour. Fortunately, the capacities we have developed as social actors can give us such access. As participant observers we can learn the culture or subculture of the people we are studying.          (Hammersley and Atkinson, 1983: 7)

Critics of the 'naturalist' perspective question the reliability, validity and generalisability of the data and findings resulting from ethnographic type research. First, as participant observation methods do not employ explicit and standardised procedures that can be replicated across a number of settings and against the same set of facts; many have subsequently argued that the results it 'produces are subjective, mere idiosyncratic impressions that cannot provide a solid foundation for rigorous scientific analysis' (Hammersley and Atkinson, 1983: 2). Second, the influential role of the participant observer—specifically via potential error precipitated by researcher effects on the situation studied—and fact that such studies are likely to take place in single, small-scale settings with limited numbers of participants again raises questions around the reliability, and generalisability of both the data and findings.

In addition to the scientific versus naturalist research debates are those intra-ethnographic disagreements around 'realism' and 'relativism'. For some, the goal of ethnography is to 'discover and represent faithfully the true nature of social phenomena' (Hammersley, 1992: 44). Yet, this perspective ignores the potential impact that the researcher has upon the collection and interpretation of 'social facts'. In contrast, others point out that there are 'social and historical constraints on what can be claimed as truth' (Scheurich, 1997: 34) and as such social worlds and so-called 'realities' are no more than 'constructs'. Consequently, through their own actions and interpretations ethnographers create social worlds, as opposed to just capturing the truthful essence of some independent social phenomena. It is nevertheless possible to cut through many of the above either-or discourses about the relative 'merits' and 'flaws' of ethnography by placing reflexivity at the centre of the practice of social research. Therefore 'rather than engaging in futile attempts to eliminate the effects of the researcher' (Hammersley and Atkinson,

19  The 'naturalist' perspective here refers to the social research concept of 'naturalism' (see amongst others Blumer, 1969; Matza, 1969; Hammersley and Atkinson, 1983).

1983: 17), we should systematically attempt to reflect upon our pivotal role within the research process. Furthermore, by adopting a more subtle form of realism, ethnographers necessarily become more circumspect with regard to the possible dangers of error:

> Ethnographers have become increasingly concerned with ways of checking their conclusions. Subtle realism simply encourages greater concern with this ... What is implied by subtle realism is not then a complete transformation of ethnographic practice. We must still view people's beliefs and actions as constructions, and this includes their accounts of the world *and* those of researchers. At the same time, though, we should not assume that people's accounts are necessarily 'true' or rational in their own terms.                    (Hammersley, 1992: 53)

Ethnography, with participant-observation at its core, is central to this study because it is the most suitable research method for documenting—from a more holistic perspective—the life styles and life chances of groups of young people 'growing up', in impoverished multi-ethnic urban neighbourhoods. Furthermore, it is only as a result of the deployment of ethnographic techniques that allow for the establishment of 'long-term relationships based on trust can one [then] begin to ask provocative personal questions, and expect thoughtful, serious answers' (Bourgois, 1995: 13). As highlighted by Karen McCarthy (2001) in her ethnographic text, the 'reality' and 'truth' of this study is that it incorporates both the stories of the young people featured and my particular way of telling them.

*Semi structured tape recorded interviews: Issues and dilemmas I*

I selected for interview (via tape recorder) twenty-two young people (See Table 3.1), with each taped interview lasting from between 60 to 120 minutes. Most of the young people were interviewed individually (all of the males, except two individuals) whereas all of the young women (except one individual) were interviewed in pairs.

Table 3.1 Tape-recorded interviews, by ethnicity and gender

|             | African Caribbean | Mixed Parentage | White | Indian | Total |
|-------------|------------------|-----------------|-------|--------|-------|
| Young Men   | 9                | 1               | 3     | 1      | 14    |
| Young Women | 4                | 0               | 3     | 1      | 8     |

The selection of young people for tape-recorded interview was not a scientific process, in that I did not choose the informants on the basis that they (as a sample) were representative of a wider 'universe of actors ... culture ... or other units under study and, therefore, could provide reliable information about that universe as it existed at a particular time' (Honigmann, 1982: 77). Whilst I endeavoured to make sure that the young people whom I selected for interview were largely representative of the wider neighbourhood youth population—taking particular account of gender and ethnicity; in truth I engaged in what can only be described as 'opportunistic sampling' (see, Honigmann, 1982; Riemer, 1977). Whenever I asked individual young people if I could interview them, most of them would say 'yes' and then go on to agree a date, time and place where it could be held. Invariably many of these potential informants would, understandably, forget to turn up. Others, like all of the Arms House Crew, point blankly refused my request for interview, whilst they were more than happy to talk at length to me about most topics, as soon as I mentioned 'tape-recorder' they would abruptly end the conversation. I soon realised that in order to interview those interested young people, I had to be opportunistic and strike whilst the 'iron was hot', so to speak. Consequently, whenever and wherever I requested an interview with a potential young informant, I had to make sure that I had my tape-recorder near-to-hand along with plenty of spare batteries and blank cassettes.

All of the tape-recorded interviews followed the same structure, with the informants being asked a number of open-ended questions that related to eight key areas of their lives. The eight identified key areas or theme headings included: neighbourhood attachments and social networks; homelands and racial/ethnic and national identity; friends and peer groups; music, clothes and other leisure activities; schooling; post-16 education, training and employment; kinship networks and home-life and lastly; crime and the police. The themes were decided upon as a result of either my own theoretical concerns—notably with youth transitions and youth sub-cultural formation—as well as those issues and concerns that I had found to be pertinent to the young people themselves; as a result of my 'kotching' with and talking to my informants during the initial stages of the fieldwork. Whilst the interviews were loosely structured around the above eight key themes, each young person was equally free to discuss anything that they felt was pertinent and central to their own lives. Consequently, whereas some informants discussed in detail the importance of music and 'raving' to their lives, others similarly spoke at length of their experiences of school or their relationships (or lack of them) with their parents and other family members.

During my time in the field I was able to use the tape-recorded interview situation to further explore themes and issues that continually were being thrown up as a result of my direct observations of, and informal conversations with, the young people. The process enabled me to cross-reference and validate information, as I was tending to find that much of the information that was being relayed to me by an informant within one particular setting (tape-recorded interviews), was being validated and substantiated by other informants in quite different settings—'on road'. There was one particular informant who was notorious amongst his peers for the creation and embellishment of 'fanciful' stories. This particular young person had made particular statements during the course of the interview session, much of which I later found out to be untrue. I was able to question much of what I had been told by this young person during the interview, through subsequent conversations with this particular young man (which took place in different settings to that of the tape-recorded interview session) as well as with his friends.

All of the tape-recorded interviews with the informants were held at the youth club, in a free room that offered privacy but that was still visible (via glass doors and windows) to other users of the building. Many researchers have undertaken interviews with young people in the privacy of either the informants' home (the bedroom), or in the interviewers' home (see Back, 1996; McNamee, 1998; McDowell, 2001), I tended to avoid such situations so as to minimise the risk of 'accusations of improper behaviour'. Nevertheless, I did undertake some interviews in my informants' homes (all took place within family living rooms), but only when interviewing a young person together with their parent(s).

### Participant observation: Issues and dilemmas II

As stated above, underpinning much of this study is a theoretical consideration of the school-to-work (or dole/crime) transitions of selected groups of young people growing up in Manor. I was concerned with exploring the informants' experiences of school and (if relevant) their post-16 choices and opportunities—or lack of them. Amidst this youth transitions theoretical framework was a further interest in exploring the intricate and complex ways that the informants govern their own lives; particularly when self-governance evidently contradicts (as in case of Arms House Crew) the mainstream values of school and wider society. Participant-observation techniques provided me with the perfect tools with which to attempt to document and explore the many ways that the informants attempt to live their lives, in spite of the influences of family, schooling, and wider political economic conditions.

As a detached/street-based youth worker, I was quite familiar (unconsciously) with many of the participant-observation ethnographic techniques that I would subsequently employ in this study. During the years that I had been working in Manor, prior to commencing field work, I had 'kotched' (as part of my role as an informal educator) with young people in a variety of settings including bars and clubs, on residentials and day trips out of town, as well as visiting many of the young people and their parents in their homes. When I began this study my role and relationship with the young people (who would become my informants) became somewhat complicated by this additional new role. There have been a number of ethnographic studies where the researchers adopted the role of youth worker in order to access potential informants (see Parker, 1974; Ackers, 1985; Back, 1996). In my case, I was a youth worker turned ethnographer, and sought to make use of the strong relationships that I had built up over the years with many of the young people (and their parents). Many writers take the view that the best 'qualitative researchers are those who are already empirically literate, that is, already familiar with the phenomenon and setting under study' (Roseneil, 1993: 189). Indeed, an ethnographer can derive distinct advantages through the exploitation of their own in-depth first hand knowledge, personal histories and 'situational familiarities as sources of research ideas and data' (Riemer, 1977: 467). Without doubt my detailed prior knowledge of the research site enabled me to quickly identify informants that might provide me with detailed and meaningful information; particularly around those more complex, nuanced—and at times subterranean—ways in which many young people attempt to govern their own lives.

Nevertheless, I was aware that there were particular ethical and moral dilemmas that I faced, which were quite distinct from the obvious participant observer-subject issues. During my time as a youth worker in Manor, I had built up a great deal of trust between myself and the local community. If a parent was having particular difficulties with one of their children (with whom I was in regular contact) they would tend to contact me in order that I might intervene, offer advice, or refer them on to a specialist agency. Similarly, many of the young people sought my advice and support around a wide range of issues, subjects and personal problems, regardless of the sensitive or intimate nature of the disclosure. Consequently, when I asked potential informants to participate in this study (apart from the issues outlined above concerning tape-recorded interview sessions) all readily agreed. In truth they were happy to participate because I had asked them and they trusted me. Many of the young people agreed to my interviewing and 'kotching' with them (which was not unusual anyway given the fact that I was a youth worker) for the purposes of this study, without even bothering to ask me what the study was actually about, or enquiring as to what was going to happen to the information.

The difficulty then arose when I was party to sensitive information and I was not sure whether I was privy to it because I was Anthony the trusted youth worker, or Anthony the ethnographic researcher. Whilst I was always honest and upfront about my role as a researcher and explained to the informants that I was undertaking research with them in order to explore and document their experiences as young people growing up in Manor, I felt that in most cases they did not fully understand. As far as the young people were concerned they were 'helping out' Anthony to write a book about 'us, the youth of Manor'. For my part, I was not always sure when I was Anthony the youth worker and Anthony the ethnographer. On many occasions whilst interviewing the young people, if particular issues or problems arose as a result of the questions, I would automatically find myself going into youth worker-advice worker-counsellor mode.

Even so, being employed as a neighbourhood youth worker afforded me excellent opportunities to observe the young people within a wide variety of informal settings. Many of my observations took place in the youth club and around the numerous public spaces within Manor where it was common for groups of young people to congregate (see chapter six). Furthermore, as I lived in a neighbourhood that bordered onto Manor, I regularly saw my informants in 'our' local chip shop, shopping centre(s), cinema, bars and pubs. I would not say that I 'hung about' with my informants, but rather that my role as a youth worker and the fact that I lived in very close proximity to their neighbourhood, allowed me to come into regular and natural contact with many of my informants. This last fact was very important, particularly with regard to the Arms House Crew who would have found it difficult to have me 'hanging about' with them 'on road'—like I was part of their crew—for the purpose of my research. It was much easier for me to see them in the youth club, local pub, or at a rave and then naturally spend time 'kotching' and 'catching joke' with them. As a result of the trust that I had managed to build up with the young people over the years, I was able to obtain a lot of honest and detailed information about the informants that perhaps other researchers might not have been able to access.

During the initial stages of the participant observation process, I tended to just observe those young people who attended the youth club or 'hung about' in other public neighbourhood settings. At the end of each day I would then write up my observations in my fieldwork journal. The selection of young people therefore, as was the case with the tape-recorded interviews, was again very much reliant upon those 'opportunist research strategies' (Riemer, 1977) that I was able to draw upon as a result of my familiarity with my informants and research site. Consequently, I was only going to observe those young people who were happy to attend the youth club, and who tended to 'hang about' in public spaces in the neighbourhood. Those young people who stayed in their homes all the time, or who 'hung about' in different neighbourhoods would invariably not feature very much in this particular study.

## A dichotomy of practice: Youth work and ethnography

As hinted at previously there were major contradictions with regard my role as youth worker and that of ethnographic researcher. I had a very close relationship with many of the informants, yet the research required that I develop a certain amount of 'objective' distance. Many of my field note diary entries pertain to my concerns with the dilemmas and conflicts of my dual role. On one occasion I recount how I am watching the pups play fight in the youth club, and that I am aware that it is going to escalate out of control. As a youth worker, 'good practice' dictates that I should step in early on to diffuse the situation, before 'things' escalate out of control. Yet as a researcher I am seemingly more concerned with observing (for later documentation) the complex and nuanced interplay and actions of the main protagonists. Similarly, another entry into my fieldwork dairy detailed the emotionally draining impact of the field research process. I recorded how 'I feel like a fraud sometimes, every time I talk to someone, its like I am not interested in them, just in what they are telling me. Every question I ask is for a reason, more information to add to my data collection'. (Field work diary). Fortunately, such extreme moments of self-doubt and 'researcher fatigue' did not feature very often throughout the duration of the fieldwork process. I was able to more-or-less balance my two roles through the recording (each and every evening) of the particular issues, problems and conflicts as they arose from the field. By so doing, I was able to obtain distance from my informants by taking stock of my own thoughts, feelings and actions (as well as those of my subjects) and potential impact upon the fieldwork process.

Various ethnographers who have undertaken participant observation within community settings, have spoken about the difficulty of trying to remain neutral when working in the field (see, Gans, 1982; Jarvie, 1982; Dennis, 1993; Bourgois, 1995; Back, 1996). Indeed, the researcher invariably has to contend with numerous dilemmas and 'issues in the field to which they must respond if they are to maintain good relations with all segments of the community—and this is not always an easy task' (Dennis, 1993: 67). Within Manor there was a history of friendly rivalry that existed between those young people who lived on the Michaels Estate with those from the Arms House area. Traditionally, the Michaels Estate was renowned as a tough estate with high crime levels and 'marauding gangs' of young males who were well known to the police and the local youth courts. Similarly, the Arms House area was viewed as a tough 'place' where gangs of young males controlled their turf and cemented their 'road reputations' with violence and low-level drug dealing and other 'hustles'. By the time I began working on the Michaels Estate as a youth worker, things had calmed down considerably, due in part to the installing of a part-time 'cop shop' on the estate; but also because the younger generation of Michaels Estate (including the Grafters and the Safe Crew) were more interested in 'joy riding', and earning a living through 'grafting' (or attending college) and not in 'badness' and crime. In contrast, the young members of the Arms House area were intent upon upholding the area's notorious reputation and fastidiously sought to follow in the footsteps of their older brothers, cousins and uncles in perpetuating 'badness' (see chapter eight).

As a youth worker, and later on as a researcher, I regularly found myself unwittingly caught up in the two groups' rivalry. My relationships with many of the young people from the Michaels Estate was very strong, and had been built up over a number of years. In contrast, my relationships with the informants from the Arms House area were much newer and at times conflictual (see chapter six), due in part to the fact that Arms House crew viewed the youth centre as their 'youth club' and found it difficult to comply with the youth club rules—namely paying the twenty pence entrance fee. Whereas the Arms House crew publicly revelled[20] in the fact that they had 'stolen' the younger Michaels girls (the Poppettes) away from Grafters, the Michaels young men (Safe Crew

---

20  Members of the Arms House Crew took to hanging about the Michaels Estate with the Poppettes in full view of the Grafters.

and Grafters) would regularly and mischievously inform the Arms House Crew about the latest trips, information, 'special favours' or help that I had allegedly bestowed on them via my role as senior youth worker. On many occasions I was accused by the Arms House Crew of showing favouritism to the Grafters and Safe Crew, 'you don't tell us about nuttin Anthony, its like you don't want man's around'. Considering the tough, uncompromising stance that the Arms House Crew liked to project, I never ceased to be amazed by these many public displays of paranoia and insecurity. The Michaels young men were not averse from a spot of paranoia themselves, as there were plenty of occasions when they would accuse me of being too soft on, and showing favouritism to, the girls—firstly the Sweat Shop girls, and latterly the Poppettes.

*The ethnographic process continued: Age difference, class, locality, ethnicity, and gender.*

Whilst my experiences of growing up (as a young black male) in decaying urban neighbourhood in the Midlands provides me with useful insights with regards to some of the everyday experiences of my research subjects, it would be false of me to claim that I have 'insider' knowledge, and can therefore legitimately tell the 'truth' about my informants' lives, because of my own similar experiences. It would be equally errant of me to claim that I am more qualified for this particular study—than say a white ethnographer—because as a black male researcher I 'naturally' have a closer affinity and empathy with my black informants (Blauner and Wellman, 1973; Lawrence, 1982). Obviously, such 'truth' claims are false for a number of reasons, over and above the fact that this study is not solely concerned with black youth. As an ethnographer, I have had to work sensitively across the boundaries—not just of race and ethnicity, but also of gender, class, age difference, and locality. Even amongst my black subjects, it was not a given that I would automatically be accepted by them, solely because of our shared African-Caribbean heritage. As I discuss later on (see chapter six), the young people featured in this study illustrate the fact that there are multiple and competing black identities, making ridiculous 'essentialist' claims of the homogenous black British experience, or subject.

My beliefs, lifestyle, age, educational and occupational experiences result in my version of African-Caribbean/black British-ness, being somewhat different from individual members of the R'n'B Girls and Arms House Crew. Equally, as a male researcher I was conscious of the gender dynamics within the research process, particularly those concerning exploitation and power:

The interview process opened young women to the kinds of exploitation
that feminist critics have levelled at male researchers. Reflecting on these
events, I think a variety of dynamics occurred ... I do not think that all
my interactions with women were totally limited by the sexism that was
so widely prevalent. But neither did these relationships fully escape the
effects of gender inequality ...young women would not always be willing
to discuss areas of their private lives, and in many ways the question was
how far we could negotiate our differences.

(Back, 1996: 25)

My relationships with the young women featured in this study had been
developed over a number of years, and as such all subsequent interactions were
based upon trust and familiarity. During the interviews all of the young women
were exceptionally honest and frank about all aspects of their private lives. Some
of the male subjects on the other hand, were at times rather coy and spoke in
'general' terms about their sexual liaisons/relationships with young women. Of
course my positive relationships with the young women did not distract me from
the wider sexism that existed, and did not make me totally immune from the
power play of gender and sexuality. During one particular evening in the youth
club, I was helping one of the young women with her college work, and was
not able to jump up to immediately assist two young men who wanted me to
help them fill out their passport forms. When I had finished helping the young
woman, the two young men began 'dissing' me arguing that 'you got no time for
us, you've only got time for her cleavage'. The young woman in question had been
wearing a low cut top, and according to the young men she had been showing
'off her cleavage' and using her sexuality in order for me to help her.

Later on in this book (see chapter six), I discuss the fact that many of my
research subjects and their parents were born in Manor, or very near to it, and
had built up extensive local kinship, and friendship networks. The outcome
was that the majority of my informants exhibited strong local 'place' identities,
and therefore in normal circumstances would be quite hostile and suspicious
of 'outsiders' like myself. Particularly those outsiders who walk around their
neighbourhood holding tape-recorders and asking lots of intrusive questions. I
was able to gain access to, as well as the trust of, my informants mainly because I
was not perceived as 'an outsider', but rather as 'our youth worker'. When I initially
began undertaking youth work in Manor, there were many older groupings of
young people who viewed my presence with a certain amount of suspicion. They

would invariably enquire amongst their younger peers, as to who I was and what I was doing hanging around their neighbourhood? Even though I do not claim to be an 'insider', I was nonetheless a known 'face' within and around Manor, which in my informants' eyes gave me an attachment to their local 'place'.

## Chapter Four

# Education, employment and training

Research commissioned for the '*Bridging the Gap*' study/report (Social Exclusion Unit, 1999) suggested that the main risk factors—alongside poverty and family disadvantage—associated with non-participation at age 16-18, is educational underachievement and educational disadvantage. Analysing data from the *Youth Cohort Study* (YCS) and *Longitudinal Study of Young People in England* (LSYPE) the authors of the study note that:

> whether young people continue in education after the age of 16 is strongly determined by their GCSE attainment. Of those who did not attain five good GCSEs, a little over half stayed on in full-time education, compared to 88% of those who did.
>
> (DCSF, 2008b: 22)

The study also found that thirty-six per cent of young people who left school with no qualifications were 'Not in Employment Education or Training' (NEET) at age sixteen. Truancy and school exclusions also greatly impact upon young people's educational underachievement and non-participation in employment education or training. Statistics from the *Youth Cohort Study Report No 34* (cited in Social Exclusion Unit, 1998) found that thirty-eight per cent of truants reported that they had no GCSEs compared with three per cent of non-truants, and that those young people who miss school (either through truanting or from being permanently excluded) are more likely to be out of work at age eighteen, and statistically are more likely to become homeless. The YCS and LSYPE 2008 found that only thirty-five per cent of persistent truants continued in education at age sixteen, whilst twenty-seven per cent were NEET (DCSF, 2008a).

*Conflict and Underachievement*

In keeping with the numerous qualitative studies concerning the perennial 'problem' of working-class young males' (both black and white) educational under performance (see, Corrigan, 1979; Epstein et al., 1998; Sewell, 1997; Willis, 1977) the overwhelming majority of my male (and female) informants aged sixteen or older had left school with little or no formal qualifications. For many of the young people featured in this study school, in terms of education and learning, was viewed as a negative experience:

> *Martin:* I just go to school and do the day and go home. That's it really. I don't really enjoy it, school and that.
> *A.G.:* So there is nothing about school that you find enjoyable?
> *Martin:* No, not really. If I didn't have to learn at school and I could learn at home from my mom or something [his mother is a school music teacher] like that it would be better.

As was the case with Martin, Lazy Boy (who left school with no formal qualifications) also had nothing positive to recollect about his time spent at secondary school:

> *Lazy Boy:* The school itself was rough and the teachers weren't strict enough, not a good education I don't reckon, 'cos the teachers like they weren't really into their jobs like they should have been … it was a rubbish school really.

Sweet Boy also held negative views about his old secondary school teachers:

> *Sweet Boy:* All I really remember is how they [teachers] used to ignore certain people, they used to be like 'wait a minute and I'll be with you in a minute' and by that time they've been over and seen who they've needed to see. So now like I'm just getting up yeah [agitated] 'cos like now if there's say a kid whose like smarter than me, even if he's a little bit smarter they'll put him in front of me, and a kid that's a little bit smarter than him they'll put in front of him, and it will go on like that. Like say there's thirty kids in the class then I'll be the last person, if I'm not so smart, out of the whole class. I'll be at the end of the line.

Kanya and Darlene also held negative attitudes about their secondary school teachers:

> *Darlene:* I don't like nothing about school apart from Art. I don't like nothing, because they [teachers] just give us so much work and they just

don't care. And then they're like 'do this, do that', they expect us to do it
just like that, and I bet you any money when we go work yeah, it ain't even
gonna be like that. They don't sit down to consider, oh they're fourteen
or fifteen year old girls yeah, just trying to make a way, we're still doing
other things, like with me especially, I just do so much …

*A.G.:* What do you mean by 'so much'?

*Darlene:* Like my house, this work [voluntary junior youth leader]
my dancing, singing, group things like writing songs, all housework,
homework, my coursework, waking up to go school with this stress as
well, I hate school, can't wait to leave school.

*Kanya:* With me schools alright you know, the only thing that gets on
my nerves in school is teachers, who are so ignorant, there so stupid and
I don't know how they got jobs, well not all teachers I have to say, but I
think sometimes they can go overboard with like coursework. Like for
some weeks you might not get nothing, then all of a sudden you might
get coursework for science, then next session then, blap, blap, blap, blap
[signifying quick succession with no breathing space] you know like they
don't spread it out, they give it to you all at one time.

When my informants did speak positively about school it was usually in
relation to 'hanging about' and 'catching joke' in the classroom or at break times
with friends. In particular, many of the black informants (both male and female)
tended to bring aspects of road culture (such as 'catching joke' and the 'not having
it' 'rude boy' or 'facety black girl'[1] persona) into the classroom, which invariably
led to conflict with their mainly white teachers:

*Kanya:* I think a lot more of the black girls get in trouble, I wouldn't
say it's because they're black, a lot of them are more troublesome, not
troublesome but say louder, if they're loud then they get in trouble for
being loud. But the white people wouldn't get in trouble for being loud,
they'd get in trouble for being bad.

*A.G.:* Do you think black girls have a rougher image than say white
girls?

---

1   'Facety black girl' persona is a counter point to the 'rude boy' in road culture but plays upon stereotypical
    images of the 'mouthy' black young woman who will cut her eye at and 'cuss down' anyone who disrespects
    her. White young women who are also part of road culture will also adopt the 'facety girl' persona.

*Kanya:* No, they're [black girls] just not having it. Not image, maybe their attitude with the teachers.

*Darlene:* Mrs Henry gets sick with it though, she knows all the culture, she knows everything.

*A.G.:* What colour is she?

*Darlene:* She is black.

*A.G.:* But she doesn't act it?

*Darlene:* I think she acts too black when she's with us, she's too facety, I don't know.

*Kanya:* You know she thinks 'cos she's a black teacher she's like got to. I don't know, she's an got ok way of thinking like trying to bring more black things into assembly, she does stuff like that, but then at other times she'll try and like put black people down, not put them down but, but if there's a group of us whatever, I wouldn't say being loud but just being us you know like when we're together and that, of course we'll be louder than just one person, and she'll [black teacher] start giving us lectures about if you were being loud in an interview you wouldn't get the job, but most people wouldn't be loud in an interview, and you know like she goes on and on about rubbish, and then she wants to go and tell other teachers, she's just extra.

Darlene and Kanya furthermore discuss the important link between 'badness' schooling and 'road culture':

*A.G.:* Do you think a lot of crime is committed by black young people, more 'badness'?

*Kanya:* No, I think its a little circle thing, like they might get in trouble at school or whatever and like get kicked out, that means they're on the street and get into crime and then the police, its a vicious circle.

*Michelle:* Does it happen just with black young people, or does it happen with both? [Youth worker and second interviewer]

*Kanya:* It happens with both, but more black I think, I think there's more black people that get kicked out of school, so that means there's more black people on the street.

*Michelle:* Do you think the teachers feel that much more threatened when it's a black child being rude as opposed to a white child?

*Darlene:* Some teachers do feel more threatened.

*Kanya:* Yeah, some of 'em do, but I suppose there's school rules ennit and I suppose they've got to follow them to keep order.

*Michelle:* Would you describe yourself as being good or bad students?

*Darlene:* I would say I'm a good student but if the teacher has done something wrong to me then I will say something, like say something might happen and they might shout at the wrong person or something or accuse them of doing something. If I know that's wrong then I will say something, I do what I've got to do, sometimes I might get in trouble here and there or whatever, but I do what I got to do.

*Kanya:* I'm an alright student, I wouldn't say I'm a Rachel goody goody pupil, but I'm not a bad student I think, but the same sort of thing as Darlene actually, some of the teachers sometimes think 'cos like you're a student and that, they think they can do whatever and that they can get away with it, 'cos a lot of us we stand up to the teachers and say whatever, and a lot of the other people they don't say anything, they know the teachers been bad and that, but they just shut out their ears, and that's why us lot get in trouble more than other people 'cos we don't take it.

As discussed in chapters 6 and 7, an important aspect of road culture for the young people is the 'not having it' attitude, which is a refusal to be seen as a 'pussy' or an idiot who others will prey on. Conflict ensues in school for many of the young adherents of road culture as they are not prepared to be 'disrespected' by rude adult teachers, and so argue back.

*A.G.:* So basically black kids don't take no shit from the teachers?

*Darlene:* We're only saying what has to be said at the end of the day.

*Kanya:* Yeah, and if they don't like it then they try and say [oh you've got a bad attitude] du du du du, back chat, but its not always that, its just sometimes they just don't listen they're too fast[2].

*Darlene:* They think 'cos we're kids they can take advantage of us because we're younger, and we're this and we're that, and they're the adults they know everything, in that respect they're so thick.

It is important to note that whilst black young people are more than likely to be in dispute with their teachers, those white young people who are heavily

---

2   'Fast' here refers to the teachers being meddlesome or troublesome, in that they go out of their way to look for confrontation with certain pupils.

involved in road culture are also more than likely to find themselves in regular conflict with teachers:

> *Charley:* I didn't really like school. I just didn't think that they [teachers] treated me very fairly.
>
> *A.G.* Why was that?
>
> *Charley:* Because of my sister, she was like a good student, a well-spoken brainy individual, and where I might be brainy I don't really show it. Whereas she was the type of person to get her work done on time and that, see I can learn and take things in very quickly, but my sister she just has to read it once and she'd know it, and they expected me to be the same. Like she was really quiet and I was like loud and mouthy and they just expected me to be exactly like her and I'm not basically. So I didn't really like school at all.
>
> *A.G.* So were you and all your friends seen as loud and disruptive by the teachers?
>
> *Charley:* With my black friends we was disruptive, but when I went into the fourth going on fifth year, I was with a group of girls that school would class as decent you know like straight A students.
>
> *A.G.:* Why do you think that you and your black friends were quite disruptive, was it to do with black culture?
>
> *Charley:* Well I just think it was personally how we all clicked together. Like individually we were all good, but when we got together we just wound each other up, and end up outside the headmistress's office and that, but that's just how we were, we used to wind each other up.

Whilst many of the black young women in this study talked about the ongoing conflict between themselves and their white teachers, unlike their male peers, it did not result in them being excluded from school or under-performing academically to the same degree as their black male peers. Research also indicates (Fuller, 1984; Mac an Ghail, 1988) that whilst black female pupils display strong anti-school attitudes, at the same time they also manage to place a high value on educational achievement. In contrast to their female peers, black male students tend to create anti-school and anti-education subcultures (see Majors, 2000; Parry, 1996; Sewell, 1997), which result in them being more likely to be suspended or permanently excluded from school in comparison to their white or Asian peers (Gillborn and Gipps, 1996; Gillborn and Mirza, 2000).

Tall Boy was one such young black male who was constantly in conflict with his teachers and had been suspended from school on numerous occasions. On one occasion Tall Boy turned up at the youth club looking rather sorry for himself. I asked him 'what was up with him' and he replied that he had been suspended from school that day. Apparently he wore trainers in school, when the school rules clearly stated that students had to wear shoes at all times except during P.E and games lessons. Tall Boy had just finished P.E. [physical education] but could not be bothered to change back into his shoes, so as he was walking through the corridors the Deputy Head Teacher informed Tall Boy that he should not be wearing trainers and then physically went to remove the trainers from Tall Boy's feet. Tall Boy resisted and in the ensuing mêlée accidentally kicked the Deputy Head Master. Tall Boy was subsequently suspended for one week. It was no surprise therefore to hear him describing his teachers as 'idiots' who fail to show students any kind of 'respect':

> *Tall Boy:* Teachers are idiots, I wouldn't mind teachers if they showed us respect but they feel they don't have to show us any respect, it's like for instance, when I went on my work experience yeah, my teacher must of said I got one of the best reviews for the whole thing and she said if I could speak to them [workers and supervisors at the work placement] in a manner and be nice to them and everything like that, why can't I be nice to the teachers, 'cos we was having like a discussion about in assembly and they were like asking me questions, so I just said 'cos they [people at work placement] showed me respect which you teachers have never shown us, I got suspended for that.
>
> *A.G.:* You got suspended for saying that?
>
> *Tall Boy:* Yeah, 'cos I was rude about it, I said to her the difference between them and yous lot [teachers] is that they know how to treat people with respect, their not just dam rude and stuff like that and because they showed me respect, I showed them respect back, and she [teacher] then tried to stop me but I must have cut her out and I kept speaking, and all the children started cheering and everything like that. I got suspended for a day.
>
> *A.G.:* So would you say you're a bad student or a good student?
>
> *Tall Boy:* I correct the teachers and put them right and it makes them angry. They will say 'I told you to do this' and 'I asked you to do that' and I'll say 'you never asked me, you tell me, if you'd have asked me, you'd have

said please or something like that'. When they make mistakes I correct
them and they start getting angry and it goes on from there.

A.G.: Do you think that perhaps if you just put up with it then maybe
you'd have an easier life in school?

*Tall Boy:* That's the thing I can't put up with it makes me angry, I have
before and it just stores up bare anger in me 'cos of the way they talk
to you and everything. I told my mom and she just said I'm not gonna
be there that much longer anyway. When I get to college its gonna be
different in college 'cos they give you respect in college.

Whilst Tall Boy had been temporarily suspended on numerous occasions,
there were a number of young men featured in this study who had been
permanently excluded from school. Raymond had been permanently excluded
from two secondary schools and Simon Peter's permanent exclusion (which
came about through him pulling out a knife on a male teacher and threatening
to kill him) only helped to propel him even further into a life of drug taking
(and selling crack cocaine), violence and robbery.

## School regrets and post-16 choices

Many of the young people featured in this study who had left secondary school,
whilst admitting that they had disliked school (in particular the disrespectful
attitudes of certain teachers), they also acknowledged their regret at leaving the
education system aged sixteen with little or no academic qualifications. During
one particular day in August (just after the GCSE results had been released)
at the Youth Centre, members of the Pups and the R'n'B girls were discussing
their recent GCSE results. Nathaniel entered the conversation and said how
proud he was of his younger brother who had recently obtained eight GCSE
passes at A-C. Nathaniel had promised to buy his younger brother some designer
garms[3] if he got his GCSEs. I then asked Nathaniel why he had not held such
high educational expectations for himself. At first Nathaniel said that school
was not for him and that he was not an 'education type person', as his place was
'on road and not in no book learning'. After a short while Nathaniel regretfully
explained that he was unable to take his GCSE exams because at the time
he was on remand in Feltham awaiting trial for an aggravated robbery charge.
Consequently, it messed things up for him academically. I asked him why he
had never gone back to school or college in order to re-take his GCSEs or other

3   Garms refer to garments, clothes.

qualifications, but he just replied that it was a 'long thing' and that it was too late for him now. Instead, since leaving school Nathaniel had earned money from 'hustling on road', sporadic temporary employment in a local authority Housing Office (which he obtained through his aunt) and since turning eighteen has been on the income support merry-go-round[4]. Many of the other informants were even more open with regard to their regrets around their lack of formal qualifications and subsequent post-16 choices:

> *Kandy:* I was meant to go to St.. Saviours Secondary School.
> *A.G.:* But you didn't used to go?
> *Kandy:* No, and my mom was fined three times. I hated school, but if I could go back I would behave so much, I'd sit down and do my work, I'd do my exams I'd do my work ... Yeah, I'd do my homework everything, I'd behave so much. There was this one girl in my class and when we I used to be with her I'd play up, I'm not saying it was her 'cos it was me, I used to be naughty all the time, they used to say to me 'oh, do your work' and I would say 'what's the point', but it it if I could go back now.
> *A.G.:* Why couldn't you see the point of doing your school work back then?
> *Kandy:* Nah, I used to think well I'm gonna get a job no matter what, but I was wrong.
> *A.G.:* What kind of job did you want?
> *Kandy:* I want to work in an office, but then I wanted to be a solicitor, but that's nang[5].

Eddie also felt that perhaps if he had knuckled down, as opposed to acting the class clown, and got his GCSE passes it would have afforded him more career options in later life:

> *Eddie:* Loved school for what it represented, but I didn't like school for what they tried to teach me, I didn't get on with the teachers 'cos I was the class clown. I didn't get on with the teachers 'cos I'd just do what I

---

4   Income support merry-go-round is where young people who are aged 18 or older sign on for state benefits for six months or more until they are then requested to attend a job search course or undertake a government sponsored work-based training scheme like New Deal. In order to avoid being forced to partake in New Deal or Job Search the young person will sign off and then sign back on again a couple of months later.

5   Nang is a steet term for rubbish, crap or stupid.

liked, and I mean for the benefit of the tape [tape recorder] which most people won't know, I came out of school with no qualifications, nothing. A lot of people say to me [you're educated you're clever] but you know it's not necessarily important to have your GCSEs but it's a nice option you know. I think it gives you more options in life, you realise that after you've got out there [big wide world] and learnt and you've worked, you think to yourself I could have got a nice job with just three A-Cs, I could be sitting down in a nice warm office doing next to nothing, now I've got to do this. Don't get me wrong, I love my job [fork lift driver] and love what it represents and all the rest of it, but things could have been a lot easier at this age you know what I mean. I could be in a twenty grand a year job now and not half of that or three quarters of that. I mean I'm not saying that if I'd have got all my GCSEs I'd have got the best job in the world, 'cos I could still have ended up in the same place, but I think I would have had more options to do more of the things that I would have wanted. But it's not so easy now, I mean I got a few things under my belt, got a fork lift license, I've got product knowledge, got years of experience at my work place and I'll probably move up if I keep going, which I've been told, but whether or not it happens is another thing.

*A.G.:* Do you regret not getting any GCSE passes at A-C?

*Eddie:* I used to regret not having 'em and I wish I did have 'em. I don't regret, I just wish I had them and that they was there, but regret is something that can eat you up and turn you inside out if you really think about it.

*A.G.:* Have you thought about going back to college or anything?

*Eddie:* I went to college and studied a few things like English and that, and I thought why am I torturing myself, what is it that I am trying to prove? What is the actual reason that why I'm going to college, is it that I'm going to college to get these A-Cs 'cos I want this certain job, or am I going back to college to prove to people that that I've got an education? And at the time it was to prove to people that I've got an education.

Similarly, Melinda also wished that she had worked harder in school and not spent her days there gossiping about boys, clothes and whatever else was happening 'on road' outside of school:

*A.G.:* What were the teachers like in your school?

*Ayesha:* Teachers are teachers, they give as good as they get, like you be rude to them and they be rude to you, they then try and be more rude 'cos they can, 'cos they're teachers and that, but sometimes you just don't have it, but still you sometimes have to know when to stop.

*Melinda:* I wish I'd have listened to 'em now ennit.

*Ayesha:* Teachers weren't really horrible to me.

*Melinda:* They were horrible to me.

*A.G.:* Why was that?

*Melinda:* 'cos I didn't do the work or anything, but I wish I'd done it now, yeah I wish I'd done it now.

*AG:* [to Ayesha] Did you do all your work?

*Ayesha:* When I was with her [Melinda] we didn't work like, but when she never came in I used to do my work.

*Melinda:* 'cos we used to talk all the time.

*Ayesha:* We used to have loads of things to talk about, 'do you know what happened last night' and 'he rang me' and 'this happened like' and that's all we used to do for the whole lesson, but when she weren't there [Melinda] I used to do all my work.

*A.G.:* [to Melinda] So why did you wish you had listened to your teacher?

*Melinda:* 'cos I wish I would've went to college, wish I would've got better grades and all that.

*A.G.:* But couldn't you have still gone onto college after you left school?

*Ayesha:* She could have but she didn't want to.

*Melinda:* I could have went but I thought I was gonna find a job and have dough[6] and that, but I haven't.

*A.G.:* What job did you want?

*Melinda:* I don't know, in a shop, but I can't even get a job in a shop.

*A.G.:* You've tried then?

*Melinda:* Yeah a few times, but no one wants me.

A number of recent studies have similarly found that many young people had wished that they had worked harder when they had attended secondary school (see, Berthoud, 1999; Lloyd, 1999; Fitzgerald, Finch and Nove, 2000; Aymer and Okitikpi, 2001).

---

6   Dough here refers to 'money'.

## Goin' college

The majority of young black men in this study will on leaving school at sixteen either enrol on a full time vocational type course at a college of further education—in addition to obtaining part time paid employment within the 'clean' service sector—or else endeavour to make a full time career 'on road' perpetuating 'badness'. All of the black female informants attended full time college courses, but were more evenly split between academic and vocational study, as well as having part time paid employment. In contrast all of the white young male (and the majority of white young female) informants had on leaving school at sixteen found (or attempted to find) paid full time employment as labourers and semi-skilled manual workers (in the case of the young men), or as factory workers and/or shop assistants (the case with the young women). During the last thirty years or so, whilst the youth labour market has virtually collapsed, young people's participation rates in post-compulsory education have more than doubled. The proportion of 16-18 year-olds in England in full time education has increased from 34.9 per cent in 1988 to 63.2 per cent in 2007 (DCSF, Statistical First Release 13, 2007).

The rapid increase in rates of participation by 16-18 year-olds in post-compulsory full time education was fuelled by a combination of factors. First, the introduction of the GCSE final year examination—which also incorporated assessment through coursework—in the mid 1980s that helped raise levels of attainment across the board for those young people completing their secondary education (see, Ashford et al., 1993; Gray et al., 1993). Second, the collapse of the youth labour market coupled with the withdrawal of state benefits compelled many 16-18 year-olds to stay on in full-time post-compulsory education (Ashton et al., 1990; Furlong, 1992; Hollands, 1990; MacDonald, 1997). Third, reforms in the further education sector resulted in the broadening out of the curriculum to include more vocational and foundation courses and so 'lessening the perception that education is an option reserved only for an academic elite' (McVicar and Rice, 2001: 2). Last, the wholesale expansion of higher education resulted in lower entry requirements, 'thereby increasing the probability of entry into higher education for those individuals who complete further education' (McVicar and Rice, 2001: 9).

As stated earlier in this book, on leaving secondary school the vast majority of the young black informants would subsequently enrol on a full-time vocational course at a college of further education. Raymond, who had been permanently excluded from two previous secondary schools, at sixteen embarked upon a full time NVQ Foundation course in Electronic Engineering. Sweet Boy was studying full time on an intermediate Level Media Production course, as well as re-taking his GCSEs in Maths and English. Griot had attended college full time for three years studying Information Technology from Foundation (NVQ) right through to Advanced Level (GNVQ). Even Eddie who is part of the Grafters Crew initially attended college on leaving school but dropped out after feeling that he was going to college for the wrong reasons. Darlene studied for her Advanced Level (GNVQ) in Performing Arts, Kanya undertook three A-Levels in Psychology, English and Law, whilst Ayesha took a course in Leisure and Tourism. Although the Pups were all in secondary school throughout the entire period that I undertook my field work, I subsequently discovered that the majority of black members had since enrolled on a variety of full-time college courses ranging from Business Studies, I.T. right through to Electronic Engineering. Evaluating YCS and LSYPE Cohort Study statistics for England 2007 participation rates for 16 year-olds in full time further education are significantly lower for young white males/females (sixty-nine per cent) than for young people from other ethnic backgrounds; ninety per cent of black and Asian young people were in full time education at age 16 (DCSF, 2008a)

Whilst it is true to say that there have been substantial increases in the numbers of young people participating in post-compulsory further education—with higher than average participation rates amongst black and minority ethnic young people, as illustrated within this study—according to a report by the Audit Commission-OFSTED (1993, as cited in Coles, 1995: 52) more than one-third of those students enrolled on a full time college course will fail to complete their studies either as a result of leaving early or because they failed their examinations and/or written assessments. During the period of my fieldwork, both Sweet Boy and Raymond had enrolled on vocational full-time college courses—whilst undertaking various paid part time employment opportunities—and subsequently failed to complete their studies. Raymond was studying for a NVQ in electronic engineering, and on his course were mainly older white males as well as two of his black male friends from school. Raymond was dyslexic and found it difficult to complete his assignments especially since he preferred to mess about during his lectures rather than pay attention to what he was being taught. Throughout the period that he was attending college, Raymond would regularly come into the youth centre and ask me to help him with his written assignments. On one such occasion Raymond came into the youth centre one evening and said 'Ant I need you to help me', he had a half written assignment in his hand and continued his dramatic plea for help 'Ant, this is serious you got to help me 'cos if I don't do well in this assignment then they'll probably throw me off the course'. He said that he would have asked his mom to help him but he did not think that she would understand much about Electronic Engineering, I replied 'I don't know nothing about electronics myself'. I then asked him why he did not ask his tutor for help? Raymond responded by saying that his tutor only speaks to the first five older white students who sit at the front of his lecture classes.

Raymond found it very difficult to concentrate for more than five minutes at a time. As we were working on his assignment he would periodically jump up and involve himself in the youth club banter or else start chasing a member of the Pups around the building—anything but focus on his assignment. I would then say to Raymond that whilst I was happy to help him to write his assignment, I was not prepared to write it for him, he would then say 'nah Ant, I know that, I just want you to put some of them big words in it for me, you know to make it sound good'. I would then spend the rest of the time spelling long words for Raymond, which he would use in his assignment. The class notes that we were working from were obviously not Raymond's as he himself could not understand the written short hand. After Raymond had phoned one of his college friends he was finally able to make sense of the class notes and proceed on to write the assignment.

On a further occasion when Raymond came into the centre in order for me to help him with his college work, he explained to me that his tutor feels that Raymond and his friends are disruptive and rude. Raymond and his two black male friends sit at the back of the class and talk loudly and crack jokes (dissing) usually at the other students (who are older and white) and at the tutor's expense. Raymond whilst acknowledging the fact that he is disruptive maintained that he was the only one of his college crew who actually did his work (assignments) because he argued at the time that he wanted to progress onto the two year advanced (GNVQ) course in Electronic Engineering. In class, Raymond said that he would talk to the white tutor sarcastically, and responded to a question with 'yeah mate'. The tutor then would say 'you are not my mate'. Raymond would continually talk to his tutor abruptly and sarcastically in order to make 'the white teacher look stupid'.

Toward the end of Raymond's first year in full-time post-compulsory education he was suspended from college (pending an investigation) for allegedly head-butting a fellow student. Even though Raymond was eventually admitted back into college one month later, during the period of his suspension he fell further behind with his college course work at a particularly crucial time of the academic year. Raymond's suspension was to have long term consequences in that, whilst he managed to eventually pass the course, he did not obtain enough credits to proceed onto the next (more advanced) level course in Electronic Engineering. Raymond subsequently enrolled on an intermediate level vocational course in I.T./Media Technology but was to drop out of that course some six months later.

During Sweet Boy's final year of compulsory education he managed to obtain a provisional place at college on an advanced level (GNVQ) two year Diploma in Media Production. In order to enrol on that particular course Sweet Boy needed to attain five GCSE passes at grades A-C. In fact he did not manage to obtain any A-C GCSE passes and so had to enrol on the intermediate level Media course instead, as well as re-taking GCSE English and Maths. After a few months of going to college Sweet Boy started missing lectures and fell behind with his course work. Where Raymond would regularly attend his classes (albeit to be disruptive) Sweet Boy spent more time at college involved in extra curricular activities. Consequently, Sweet Boy would skip lessons and spend time hanging around college with his new girlfriend (Tasha) whom he had recently met through college. Sweet Boy already had a girlfriend from 'road' but was according to him 'loved up' with this nice new black girl (Tasha) who was 'wifey material'.

When Tasha discovered that Sweet Boy was messing around with other girls, she dropped him leading Sweet Boy to reminisce about how he had stupidly 'messed things up with Tasha'. As well as the distraction of his complicated love life, Sweet Boy was also having to deal with the stress of an imminent court case to deal with. Sweet Boy and Raymond had been driving around with no licence, tax disc, or insurance and were stopped by the police. Raymond who was in the passenger seat managed to give a false name and address, whereas Sweet Boy was not so lucky. Halfway through his studies Sweet Boy was eventually thrown off his Media Production course as a result of poor attendance at classes as well as his failure to submit any coursework. He did not bother to enrol on any further college course and instead drifted in and out of part time and full time employment including stints as a PowerGen sales agent, play leader and special needs support worker.

Raymond and Sweet Boy were not the only young black males who failed to complete their college studies. Will, Eddie, Tall Boy and dj Wildstyle similarly— for a variety of different reasons—all dropped out early of their chosen courses of study. In contrast, all of their black female peers persevered with their college studies, as have many of the Pups. Griot completed his three years of full time post-compulsory education studying Information Technology and was supposed to attend a university course. Griot is an individual who is renowned 'on road' for being economical with the truth. Whereas there is no dispute that Griot completed his three years of study no one can be certain exactly what his final results were. Griot had been telling me for many months during his final year of study, that he had obtained a place at Brunel University to study for a HND in I.T. According to Griot he was 'thrown off' his HND course at Brunel University because he got into 'beef with some Asian boys from up West' on his first day, and was subsequently permanently thrown off the campus. I can only take what Griot told me (and what he also told his friends) at face value, my only reservation being that in the six or so years that I have known him, I have yet to hear of him getting into 'beef' with anyone.

## Goin' graftin'

As already discussed earlier (see chapter two) the East London has been particularly affected by the major changes wreaked (economic recession and high rates of structural unemployment) through the restructuring of the global economy and continued de-industrialisation. The groups in East London that have been hardest hit are those unskilled and semi-skilled workers, particularly young people and those individuals from black and minority ethnic communities. Nevertheless, whilst East London has seen the demise of many of its key traditional industries—including the Docks and its many affiliated industries—during the last twenty five years or so, many of the young people featured in this study have managed to take advantage of the growing service and public sectors (young black people); whilst others (young white males) have benefited from East London's close proximity to Docklands, with its redevelopment and construction boom. As such many members of the Grafters have secured regular full time paid employment positions as unskilled labourers, forklift truck operators, builders mates or apprentice electricians on numerous City and Dockland construction sites.

## The Grafters

The Grafters are a group of predominantly white young men who reside on the nearby low rise Michaels Estate. Composed of a core group of six young men—one black, one mixed parentage and the other four white—but including up to ten additional white youths who are tightly attached to the group. This group is aged from seventeen to twenty, and is distinguished by its attitude to work. They are all (apart from one young man) committed to earning a living through 'grafting' in the building industry either as labourers or apprentice tradesmen. For such young men getting and securing a proper job is viewed as an important sign of 'manhood' and adulthood (see also Johnston, et al., 2000). Since leaving school members of the Grafters have matured a great deal, when in the past they were involved in petty crime and 'joy riding' on stolen mopeds or 'nicked' cars around the neighbourhood, now they are on the whole 'law abiding citizens'. As such despite economic re-structuring, this grouping of young men are still managing to undertake (traditional) school-to-work transitions as described in Willis' (1977) study.

The key individuals of the crew are:

*Lazy Boy*, twenty year-old male, of dual heritage parentage (half Irish/half Nigerian)

*Sick Boy, a* twenty year-old white male;

*Tony C*, an eighteen year-old white male;

*Stevie*, a seventeen year-old white male;

*Eddie*, a nineteen year old black male; and,

*Sparky*, a twenty year-old white male.

## Graftin' up the city at night—Cash-in-hand work

Even before leaving school many of the Grafters had been used to working on building sites as labourers for cash-in-hand[9] payments. The main opportunity for casual cash-in-hand work was obtained through Simon, a twenty-eight year-old Michael's Estate resident who had recently came over from Nigeria to live in London. Simon ran his own cleaning company that was contracted to clean a number of office blocks in the City and Docklands business areas outside of office hours—usually in the early hours of the morning. Simon got

.9 Cash-in-hand work here refers to paid employment that is 'off-the books', whereby the young people concerned can earn money without having to pay Income Tax or National Insurance. It also means that the young people's employers can get away with paying them below the market rate, and can evade paying employers National Insurance contributions or adhering to Health and Safety regulations in the workplace

to know the Grafters through Lazy Boy (Lazy Boy's father was Nigerian and was friends with Simon) and managed to regularly employ them as cleaners for cash-in-hand payments at the end of each shift. Simon would pick up all those young people who were interested in his van at 10.00 p.m. each night and drop them back home at 6.00 a.m. the next morning. Many of the young men (aged from fourteen-sixteen at the time) used to work for Simon 'off' and 'on', when they were short of money they would work for him, but would soon get 'pissed off' by his 'slave wages' and so refuse to work for him ever again. To get the young men back on side Simon would 'woo' them by taking them to McDonalds or by giving them money. If any of the young men were short of money they would go up to Simon's flat and ask him for money usually five or ten pounds.

Where most of the other Grafter boys soon got 'pissed off' with Simon's slave wages and long unsociable hours (all of the young people soon began to regularly complain about Simon and his behaviour), Sparky would always back Simon saying it was 'money'. As a result Sparky saw my work as affecting the boys, as they would more rather be engaging with my 'youth work' agenda rather than Simon's 'illegal' work ethic. Sparky saw the boys and particularly Lazy Boy as being immature, he could not understand why they would rather be going on residentials with me rather than making money.

The Grafters have all managed to obtain paid manual employment through their extensive social networks of family and friends (as also found by Lloyd, 1999 in his study of young men and the labour market). On leaving school Sparky originally secured full time employment as a labourer on a building site as a result of his father's contacts in the 'trade'. Within a few months of meeting his current girlfriend (when he was seventeen) Sparky managed to get taken on as an apprentice electrician working for his girlfriend's father's company. Similarly, Sick Boy managed to secure a number of full time labouring and semi-skilled manual positions through his uncles or social contacts in the local pub. Indeed the local pubs of East London serve as unofficial job centres—as well as centres of deviant/criminal activity—for many a member of the wider East London Grafter community (see, Hobbs, 1988). Whilst young black people might 'diss' the pub culture of the Grafters, when young males reach school leaving age their recreational and leisure sites shift from the 'road' to that of the pubs, where they will also gain access to information about work and other (usually illegal) moneymaking opportunities. Pamela Meadows (2001) in her overview report and analysis on the findings of a number of research projects exploring young men's experiences in the labour market during the 1990s, found that

*Growing Up Bad?*

a 'recurring theme in the research has been the findings that social networks remain one of the most important means of finding a job for young people' (Meadows, 2001: 6).

### The Sweatshop Girls and Young Moms

When I first began working in Manor, as well as having regular contacts with the Pups and the Grafters, I was in regular contact with a small group of young white women aged sixteen and seventeen who also lived on the Michaels Estate. These young women—Trish, Jodie, Kay and Minty—originally used to hang about with the Grafters when they were younger, but soon tired of their company and immaturity and begun 'hanging' around with a different set of boys from another neighbourhood. Whilst the Grafters found employment as labourers and semi-skilled manual workers on leaving school, these same young women managed to obtain full-time paid employment as machine operators in local small-scale clothes and food processing factories. These young women only managed to work for a year or two before falling pregnant and subsequently giving up their jobs in order to look after their new born babies. By the time I began to undertake the fieldwork for my research—three years after I began working as detached youth worker in Manor—I had lost all contact with these young women, only seeing them from time-to time (and stopping to talk to them) on the streets pushing their baby's buggies. I would also regularly ask members of the Grafters how the girls were doing and managed to follow their changing life circumstances from a distance.

### Clean work[10]

As already stated the black young people who attended college also tended to find part time paid employment within the 'clean' service sectors, as retail shop assistants or part-time play/youth workers. At the same time as attending college, Sweet Boy managed to obtain part-time paid employment at the youth club as a junior play/youth leader. Initially Sweet Boy had shown great enthusiasm for his newly acquired position and was an enthusiastic and diligent worker. A few months later however and Sweet Boy was starting to turn up late for work, or not bother to turn up at all. Even when he was at work Sweet Boy seemed to be lethargic and disinterested. Less than six months after he was employed at

10  Many young black men saw manual labour as poorly paid 'dirty work'. It was a 'running joke' within road culture about those labourers, electricians, and bricklayers etc 'who walk about the streets (or drink in the pub) in their dirty (soiled) work clothes after 'a hard days graftin''. Black young men like Griot and Sweet Boy sought 'clean' office and hi-tech jobs that required more 'brain power' as opposed to 'hard graft'.

the youth club Sweet Boy decided to quit his job (before the decision could be taken out of his hands, as by this point the senior youth worker was tiring of Sweet Boys antics), and set about finding full-time employment. After a short spell of NEET, Sweet Boy managed to find employment as a door-to-door sales agent for an electricity company. This job was a commission only appointment and involved a great deal of travel, on many occasions for very little financial reward. He later gave up this job and made tentative steps back into the world of part-time play work. He is currently applying for positions as a residential care worker.

Similarly, Raymond also worked part-time as paid play worker but unlike Sweet Boy Raymond was very committed to his job. Whilst Raymond would mess about in college or be disruptive in school, with regard to his paid part time positions he was professional, punctual and very diligent. So much so that Raymond is in the enviable position of having to turn down many work opportunities within the play or youth work field. Both Raymond, Sweet Boy and Darlene (who was a part time dance tutor at the youth club, whilst attending college) began their play and/or youth work careers as young volunteers (before becoming junior workers) in the youth club back when I was the Centre Manager.

Griot worked part-time in a local retail outlet that specialised in games software either for personal computers or Play Stations. Raymond would sell games to his friends at very cheap prices when his boss was not around. Indeed, after three years of employment Griot was eventually sacked after his various sales scams were discovered by his manager. On many occasions Griot and members of the Arms House Crew would ask me to help them get work as youth workers, as they saw it as an easy number where they could get paid for playing pool, table tennis or mixing on the 'decks'. On numerous occasions I would explain to them that there was more to youth work than playing pool or table tennis. They remained unconvinced—and still do to this day—as to my reasonings.

## Officially NEET but working on road

A DfEE sponsored large-scale quantitative study of black Caribbean young men's education and employment experiences found:

> lower rates of employment for black Caribbean young men than white males of the same ... This study found that 46% of black Caribbean young

men were employed at the time of interview [excluding those who work part-time whilst in full-time education]. A third of those sampled [33%] were unemployed at the time of interview. (Fitzgerald, et al., 2000: 26)

Even though the majority of the Arms House crew had neither attended college or obtained any kind of paid employment, Nathaniel had since leaving school managed to work off-and-on in a variety of office based jobs (through his aunts contacts) as a clerical assistant and office junior in the City and for a local authority housing department. After a while however Nathaniel became more and more disengaged from the formal economy and instead chose to become more embroiled in 'road life', particularly the money-making aspects of 'badness'.

As discussed in chapter seven, there are those young men who eschew the values of mainstream society and attempt to make a full-time career from perpetuating 'badness' and living 'on road'. Johnston et al.'s. study (2000) located in a North East England neighbourhood and focusing on young people, transitions and social exclusion found that those youths who regarded themselves as criminals were also more than likely to regard crime as an alternative form of work (see also, Craine, 1997; MacDonald and Shildrick, 2007).

Whilst those young people in Manor who were involved in 'badness' would not refer to themselves as 'criminals'—more like 'rude boys' or would-be 'ghetto dons'[11]—they still nonetheless viewed 'living on road' as an alternative form of work. Living on road will normally involve those particular young people (usually young men) attempting to earn money from such illegal activities as street robbery, low level drug dealing, fraud or 'robbing-to-order'[12]. Such young men will normally be those hardest to reach individuals (or status zero youth, see Williamson, 1997) who claim income support/job seekers allowance at 18 for six months or more—depending on when those in the Benefits Agency decide to write to the individual and request that they attend a Job Club or participate in a government sponsored work based training programme like New Deal. At

---

11  For those young men involved in 'badness' being a 'criminal' is viewed negatively as there is no kudos or value attached to such a term. Whereas a 'rude boy' or 'ghetto don' is about power, having the entire 'neighbourhood look up to you' or 'aspire to be like you', it is about having the right image, flashy car and loads of pretty women.

12  Robbing-to-order is where an individual (fence or middleman) will ask a rude boy or out-there-boy to specifically go and steal a particular item(s). Items can include car alloy wheels, car stereos, chequebooks, credit cards, lap top computers, mobile phones, play stations, designer clothes, wide screen televisions etc.

such critical points the rude boys[13] will voluntarily sign themselves off and stop receiving benefits and subsequently remove themselves from Benefits Agency scrutiny. Two or three months later the rude boys will sign back on again, by which point they will be eligible to claim Benefits for a further six months or so. Job Seekers Allowance for those young men 'living on road' and perpetuating badness is seen as regular small change or insurance money. Working on road can sometimes be lucrative, yet it is an unreliable source of income as the rude boys can go for weeks without making any money whatsoever from their illegal underground scams; whereas they can bank on receiving their Job Seekers Allowance every fortnight.

In Manor those young black men who decide not to study at college and work part-time[14], on leaving—or being excluded from school—and finding themselves with little or no qualifications and outside of the loop with regard to information about potential career routes or training opportunities, decide that the only real opportunities available to them are those on offer via 'road life'. Many of the those young black men from the Arms House crew (and those from Safe crew) had previously held ambitions that involved being successful within mainstream society; of being lawyers, bankers, P.E. teachers, footballers or djs playing the latest Drum 'n' Bass or Garage tunes. Between the ages of eleven to sixteen, many young black men begin to come into conflict with those agents of mainstream adult society—usually teachers and in the more extreme cases, the police and Youth Justice System—resulting in many of these individuals leaving school with little or no qualifications. While those young men like Raymond and Sweet Boy will still enrol on full time college courses, many others will become totally disillusioned with all aspects of mainstream society. Consequently, young men like Redz, Manley and Nathaniel will, after leaving school cease, to have much contact with the world outside of their immediate world, which involves badness and 'road life' in general. On occasions that I have spoken to Redz or Manley about going to college, or getting a full-time job, they argue that it's too late for them to go back to studying, or the fact that they are not prepared to get a 'shit paying job' and be bossed about by some 'racist idiot'. In reality, many of these young men lack the skills and confidence to deal with

13 The rude boys are not the only individuals who sign-off-and-on every six or so months at a time. Those individuals who perhaps work in the building trade but who are paid cash-in-hand by those contractors who operate outside of the remit of the Inland Revenue etc, will also sign on for Job Seekers Allowance, and then sign themselves off when they receive a letter from Benefits Agency inviting them to attend the Job Club.

14 For many young black men grafting (working full-time as semi-skilled or manual labourers) in the building or other industries is not viewed as an attractive career choice.

'officialdom', and are invariably suspicious of government sponsored training schemes like New Deal.

The Arm's House crew follow the same paths as other black Atlantic young males of 'low social status', in wanting to look clean and get paid by any means necessary. Such young males' status is derived from consumption and badness rather than dirty work or manual labour (see, Sullivan, 1989; Anderson, 1990; Sansone, 2003). In contrast the Safe crew whilst they flirt with the style and aesthetics of badness, they nonetheless buy into the mainstream messages about social inclusion, equality of opportunity and hyper consumption as propagated by the various official government agencies, media and cultural industries; however, the subtext to these messages is that success and hyper consumption are only available to those young people who fully participate in post-16 education and training.

**Chapter Five**

# Family and home life

In the past the academy has tended to place too much emphasis upon eurocentric bourgeois household structures, typified by the nuclear family and usually featuring a male head along with his wife and children. Those family types that have not seemingly adhered to such middle-class norms, have either tended to be ignored and/or pathologised. Indeed, working-class family life has historically been viewed as problematic and dysfunctional, with research evidence suggesting that:

> the working-class man is a sort of absentee husband, sharing with his wife neither responsibility nor affection, partner only for bed. Such a view is in the tradition of research into working-class family life … Study has been piled upon study of all the things that have gone wrong, of juvenile delinquency and problem families, broken homes and divorce, child neglect and Teddy Boys … in all this the villain is often the man. The woman is presented as struggling bravely on though worn out by her children, loaded with hardship and old before her time.
>
> (Young and Wilmott, 1957: 5)

Yet the family life that Young and Wilmott discovered in East London bore little resemblance to the dysfunctional horror stories—as portrayed in the research and writings of social philanthropists such as Booth (1889 and 1902)—that involved the bullying manual labourer, his put-upon wife and their large brood of malnourished children. As a result of inter-War social and economic changes, working-class family life, whilst not utopian, improved significantly for many. There was a declining birth rate, working hours had been reduced and regulated, housing conditions had improved; meanwhile there seemed to be some evidence of an emerging partnership between husbands and their wives. It is true to say that many of these changes have not worked a revolution' as 'the old segregation of man and woman has not ended yet' (Young and Wilmott, 1957: 11). Nevertheless, Young and Wilmott could not reconcile their findings with the stereotype of the chauvinistic (and bullying) working-class husband and father.

Within Bethnal Green, Young and Wilmott (1957) discovered the prevalence of a local kinship system where the mother was both the focal point and the 'head' of an extended family network. This family typically consisted of:

> a small cluster of families, that is, the families of marriage of the daughters and their common family of origin, and it is made up of in the main of the three generations of grandparents, parents, and children.
>
> (Young and Wilmott, 1957: 32)

The mother-daughter relationship was key particularly in poor neighbourhoods where work was tenuous and finances were tight. In such situations a wife and her young family was reliant upon the financial, emotional, and child rearing support of her immediate family—principally her mother. The prevalence and importance of extended kinship patterns within working-class communities such as Bethnal Green, contradicted the assumed hegemony—as accepted by many of those working within the social sciences—of the nuclear household structure within post-industrial Western societies. Similarly, black Caribbean household structures have never conformed to the accepted middle-class family model that emphasises the small self contained unit comprising a married couple and their offspring. As a consequence, various research studies have been undertaken (see Patterson, 1965; Cashmore, 1979; Pryce, 1979; Cashmore and Troyna, 1982; see also chapter two) that have sought to highlight the inadequacies and pathology inherent within matriarchal black Caribbean households. These studies further maintain that the innumerable social problems faced by many black British young people is a consequence of their dysfunctional family backgrounds, characterised by excessive discipline, and absentee fathers. However, the above conclusions were drawn from studies where the researchers had focused primarily upon household structures and relationships, whilst ignoring those wider transnational and inter generational kinship relationships which are key characteristics of black family life (see, Goulbourne and Chamberlain, 2001; Smith, 2001).

Goulbourne and Chamberlain (2001), having undertaken a major interdisciplinary research project exploring the *'Living arrangements, family structure and social change of Caribbeans in Britain'*, tentatively come to the following conclusions. First, Caribbean families do provide the relevant care and affection needed to successfully socialise the individual into wider civil society. Second, Caribbean 'living arrangements' in Britain replicate those found in the

Caribbean, with blood ties and lineage seemingly more important than conjugal or affinal linkages. Third, Caribbean families are more reliant upon wider kinship networks for support and lastly:

> the living arrangements of Caribbean people in Britain suggest sophisticated and strong multi-dimensional and trans-national family and communal affinities. The sense of kinship solidity across generations and the Atlantic link families, and this is an important theme in the majority of individual narratives of family members. Caribbean families in Britain must be seen as an important theme in the transnational relations and unified Atlantic world which transcend national boundaries.
>
> (Goulbourne and Chamberlain, 2001: 8)

According to Goulbourne and Chamberlain's research, the Caribbean family relies upon its trans-national connections within the trans-Atlantic for the maintenance of kinship networks and support. Furthermore, diasporic connections provide the means for the retention and transmission of important cultural practices, and promote a sense of Caribbean identity. With the exception of one individual, all of the black young people who feature in my research were born in East London, and are third or fourth generation black British. The home-life experiences and living arrangements of many of these young people seemed to reflect the 'Caribbean norms' (Goulbourne and Chamberlain, 2001) of serial parenting, high numbers of lone-parent (usually the mother) households and a relatively low (or concealed) level of male involvement within the domestic arena. Many also had a strong sense of connection to the Caribbean which was exhibited and maintained through family and kinship networks, particularly grandparents. Interestingly, the living arrangements and household structures of the black young people were not too dissimilar to that of their white and mixed parentage working-class peers. Holme (1985) and Dench et al. (2006) update Young and Wilmott's (1957) study of housing and family life in East London, both studies further indicate the plurality of household structures, including co-habiting couples, re-constituted step-families, and lone-parent (mother) households. It was 'striking how much higher was the number of families who had no relatives other than parents living in Bethnal Green' (Holme, 1985: 138), where extended local (neighbourhood based) kinship relationships had since been replaced by wider translocal/transnational kinship networks.

Whilst the living arrangements and family structures of my black informants replicate those found in the Caribbean, they equally replicate those household patterns that exist in poor working-class urban neighbourhoods throughout the United Kingdom.

## Family life and household structures in Manor

During the last twenty five years or so there have been clear and marked demographic shifts throughout Britain and in many other Western societies, with regard to family and household composition 'especially in aspects of their formation and dissolution' (Allan and Crow, 2001: 1). There can now be said to be a greater plurality of family types in existence throughout Britain (and elsewhere) as a result of marital decline, divorce, re-marriage, rise in numbers of individuals living alone, increase in lone-parent households as well as larger numbers of couples choosing to live together outside of wedlock. Feminist and post-modernist discourses have endeavoured to make sense of the changing composition of family household types, particularly the concepts of the 'self' (Giddens, 1991 and 1992) and 'individualisation' (Beck, 1992), where it is argued that individuals can break free from the shackles of the past, or whether they be prescribed gender roles for women, to make their own lifestyle choices based upon their own whims, desires and ambitions. Other commentators have cautioned against totally accepting the late post-modernity thesis on the family, and point out 'the constraints on change caused by continuing inequalities which stem from differences in economic status, ethnicity, location and gender' (O'Brien and Jones, 1996: 62). Furthermore other cultural, social and economic forces within modern society have also radically shaped individuals domestic experiences, for instance:

> aspects of economic restructuring over the last twenty years, including high levels of unemployment, greater job insecurity and reduced job opportunities for school leavers in many localities ... the development of Britain as a more mixed multi-cultural society ... and altered understandings of ... gender, sexuality, marriage, and childhood, have also fostered the emergence of divergent patterns of family experience.
>
> (Allan and Crow, 2001: 34)

The changing social and demographic trends have impacted greatly on family and household structures throughout the entire United Kingdom, including many industrialised societies, but are even more marked within East London's inner boroughs. In an earlier chapter (chapter two) I have argued that East London is a particularly complex, diverse and unique area of the United Kingdom, characterised by large minority ethnic communities (including large numbers of asylum seekers and refugees), high levels of structural unemployment, ill-health, poverty, homelessness and overcrowding. Rix (1996), drawing on the Annual Abstract of Greater London Statistics from the years 1983-1992, notes that East London boroughs had higher than average (above both the national and London averages), numbers of family households with dependent children, many of whom are under five years-old, teenage pregnancy rates, and numbers of lone-parent families.

The majority of informants (black, white and Asian) featured in this study lived within a wide variety of household types, with only a very small percentage of their number living within the 'nuclear family' setting with mom, dad and siblings. Whilst there were a few young people who lived on their own, most resided with one or other of their estranged parents, usually their mother, along with their siblings. Without doubt family life within the neighbourhood of Manor is complex, diverse and is subject to continual change. During the life span of this research many of the informants had experienced a number of changes and upheavals within their domestic environments. I first came into contact with Michael (African Caribbean male) when he was eleven years old. At the time he was living with his mother and two older sisters. Yet within the space of a few years Michael's mother had fallen pregnant and invited her boyfriend (the baby's father) to live in the family home, before the breakdown of that relationship necessitated his subsequent departure. During this time Michael's eldest sister gave birth to her own child and set up home by herself. Michael has moved out of his mother's home on a number of occasions where he has invariably gone to live with either his oldest sister or with his father and step-mother.

When I first made contact with fifteen year-old Tye he was living with his Irish mother and Nigerian father. Within a few years Tye's parents had separated with his father leaving the family home. When Tye lost his mother to cancer his father moved back into the family home. As the narratives of both Tye and Michael have shown, when young people and children experience changes in their family set ups, or family 'constitution' and 'reconstitution,' 'this is best thought of as a complex set of processes taking place over a considerable time, rather than a simple or discrete event' (Coles, 1995: 61) or as a straightforward change in household structure.

I have previously discussed (see chapter two) how the collapse in the youth labour market over the past thirty years, which, exacerbated by neo-liberal government policy, has drastically altered and elongated young people's transitions from school to the job market[1]. The extended transitional phase of youth has resulted in them having to spend longer periods of time within the education and training sectors. As a consequence many young people are more financially and emotionally dependant upon their families for increasingly longer time-scales. Interestingly, there have been a number of studies that have shown how changes in household structure (as have been experienced throughout Britain during the past two decades or so) can impact negatively on young people's key transitional phases[2].

It has been suggested that young people are more reliant upon their parents as a result of extended transitions, yet the family support available to many of them may be tenuous and not very secure. Without doubt family relationships can be placed under a considerable degree of strain as a result of changes in household structures precipitated by divorce, separation and reconstituted step families; whether through marriage of co-habitation. A sizeable minority of the young people featured in this study have at some point been forced to quit their family home as a result of problems and conflict arising as a result of a parent (usually their mother) re-marrying or co-habiting with a new partner. In subsequent chapters (see chapter seven) I will argue that family life is the one significant aspect of young people's lives that can resist what Sewell (1997) refers to as the more 'negative' aspects of black youth sub-culture, or what I term as 'road culture'. Without doubt family crisis and break-down is the single most important trigger that helps to pull a small minority of African-Caribbean young men (and their white, and mixed parentage peers) more deeply into the alternative lifestyles of the 'road'. This alternative lifestyle is characterised by the 'road' ethos of anti-schooling, crime, bullying, violence, misogyny, homophobia, hyper-heterosexuality, and the acquisition of expensive clothes, jewellery and other material items.

Nevertheless, transnational familial and kinship relationships afford black youth the opportunity to connect with a culture and a way of life that is far removed from their everyday experiences growing up in Manor. When T-Boy's grandfather came over from St. Lucia to visit his family in Britain, he had not

1   See, Ashton et al., 1990; Banks et al., 1992; Furlong et al., 1996; Furlong and Cartmel, 1997; MacDonald et al., 1997; Roberts, 1997; Jones, 1999.
2   See, Hutson and Jenkins, 1987; Kiernan, 1992; Finch and Mason, 1993; Brannen et al., 1994.

been back to England since returning home to the Caribbean nearly ten years previously. For that entire holiday period T-Boy would happily and brightly come into the youth centre continually talking about his grandfather, re-telling the stories about St. Lucia (although he himself had never visited the country) and bring into the youth centre Caribbean food that his grand father had cooked. Without doubt, the arrival of his grandfather had given T-Boy the opportunity to re-connect with a Caribbean culture and heritage that was becoming more and more distant to many third and fourth generation British born black youth. Similarly Sweet Boy, although he describes himself as black British, also feels very:

> proud to be Jamaican ... I dunno it's just in me to how I dress, the food I eat ... I'm a Jamaican and I'm proud to be from Jamaica ... I mean, I haven't actually been to the rough parts, but where I've been I liked it ... when my grandad took me to different places over there, I liked it.
>
> (Sweet Boy)

Sweet Boy has very strong views about those black young people with Jamaican/Caribbean heritage who come across as Anglicised and 'cockney'[3], usually dissing[4] them by saying 'you're not a Jamaican, there's no way that you can be a Jamaican' or 'you're not black'. This strong feeling of affection and attachment to Jamaica is derived as a result of Sweet Boy's strong relationship with his grandfather who lives in Jamaica. Yet the connections to the Caribbean and its Diaspora, as exhibited by many of the black young people in this study, are rather complex and tenuous. Whilst on the one hand many of them would find it easy to describe themselves as black, or that they were born in Britain, most of the informants found it much harder to assign themselves a solely Caribbean, or indeed British identity. Whereas Sweet Boy, T-Boy, and others held deep and fond attachments to the Caribbean, this was not necessarily the case with all of the young people:

*Tall Boy:* My mom and dad were born in Jamaica, my mom was born in Orange Field and my dad was born in Kingston.[5]

---

3   There is an assumption that black/Jamaican young people should talk, behave and dress a particular way that is different to how white young people talk, behave and dress.
4   Dissing is to disrespect or to humorously ridicule another person. through word-play.
5   Both Tall Boy's parents came to England when they were young children and so have spent all of their formative years in the United Kingdom.

A.G.: Have you been to Jamaica?

*Tall Boy:* Yeah, but I didn't like it.

A.G.: Why?

*Tall Boy:* Its too hot and the people there get on my nerves ... Plus I get bitten up every time I go there by mosquitoes. My mom's going back this year and she wants me to go back with her but I said no.

A.G.: Is she going back for good or just for a holiday?

*Tall Boy:* Just for a holiday ... I think she wants to go for six months.

When I asked Tall Boy if he felt Jamaican as his parents are from there, he matter-of-factly stated that he was simply a 'British Citizen, and that's it', he replied, 'No ... 'cos they were born in Jamaica and I was born here'.

Kanya, a young woman with family roots in Barbados, was quite clear that although she likes to visit the Caribbean for a holiday, it would be a different thing to live over there:

> *Kanya:* I like it [Barbados] for a holiday but I wouldn't go and live there ... its too different from what you know here, it's too slow, everything's just slow. I'd like to go to St. Lucia [Where her friends family are from] 'cos I haven't been there yet, see what it's like there. But I wouldn't like to go and live in the Caribbean ... anywhere in the Caribbean, yeah I wouldn't want to go and live in the Caribbean.

All of the black informants tended to assign to themselves multiple black identities that reflected their specific Caribbean heritage—which was transmitted and maintained through family and kinship ties—and their individualised experiences of being third and fourth generation black Britons. As such, depending on the black young person, when asked to describe him or herself, responses ranged from black-British, black-Caribbean, British-Caribbean through to St. Lucian and black 'other'. As Alexander found in *The art of being Black* (1996), each response was always qualified further with an additional statement that sought to emphasise the point that their initial response was not the definitive answer:

> *Will:* I see myself as British and Jamaican, a bit of both, but obviously you can't put that down on them silly little things, them forms an that, but what do they say, black UK, err I don't know about that, I dunno

how they should do it because my parents are Afro-Caribbean, or West
Indies whatever, and I was just happen to be born here ennit.
*Tall Boy:* I'm a British citizen, but that's it.
*Kanya:* Well I'm black British, but when someone asks where do you
come from I don't say England, you say where your parents are from, you
say like I'm half whatever or whatever, you don't say I'm British, that's
just rubbish you don't say things like that.
*Sweet Boy:* I'd say Caribbean or black British, but it's firstly black
British.

Tizard and Phoenix, (1993: 64) in their research noticed that some of the
young people:

> seemed to switch backwards and forwards between identifications in the
> course of the interview, while others described themselves as having a
> different racial identity in different situations.

Within this study it was also found that questions around racial, ethnic and
national identity posed to the black informants, sometimes elicited different
responses depending on the setting. When I asked the same questions to them
in the youth club where they were surrounded by their peers, the black young
people on the whole tended to assert their Caribbean identities over their British
ones. During one of the sessions at the youth centre, I asked everybody whether
or not they would describe themselves as British. Little Man replied that he
was St. Lucian whilst Mikey said he was Trinidadian. Eddie: 'I'm British [his
parents are Guyanese] but to be honest I don't feel anything, I'm just glad to be
alive and that's it'. Raymond said he was Trinidadian and very sure of that, he
was again going on about white people and being very disparaging about them,
and that there was no way that he could ever associate himself with Britain. Tall
Boy (on this occasion) just said that he was Jamaican, whilst Harry said that
he was Bajan (parents are from Barbados) and went on to further push Eddie
some more as he wanted to know whether or not Eddie felt any attachment to
the Caribbean. Harry said that he couldn't believe that Eddie could call himself
British and make no reference at all to Guyana where Eddie's parents came
from. Harry identifies with where his parents are from whilst at the same time
acknowledging that he was born in Britain. He asserted that there was no way
that he could ever support England in football, even though he is a fanatical

football fan. Harry:'I tell ya, I can't understand them black people who support England at football, or who can walk around and say that they're proud to be British ... madness'.

## Parenting in Manor I: Mothers

One of the main distinguishing features of Caribbean Diasporic family life is the unique position that is accorded to both the mother and grandmother. The significance of this is borne out by the high incidence of lone-mother households, and trans-national kinship networks that are constructed around the matriarch figure; usually the grandmother. The apparent matri-focus of many Caribbean families—with its perceived 'dysfunctionality'—has in the past been viewed by academics (Cashmore, 1979; Pryce, 1979; Cashmore and Troyna, 1982) as the main reason why black youth were prone to criminality, deprivation and social exclusion. On the other hand, there have been a number of researchers who have re-assessed the above static interpretation of Caribbean living arrangements. Goulbourne (2001) argues that the Caribbean family has always exhibited strong 'modern' or even 'post-modern' characteristics, where an individual's autonomy within the family is of considerable importance. The increasing plurality of household structures within wider society, with high incidences of lone (working) mother households and serial parenting, can be said to replicate those Caribbean norms of traditional family life.

Many of my white informants—like their black peers—also lived within lone-parent families, or were characterised by serial parenting and diversity of household structure brought about by divorce, separation or bereavement. Significantly, the majority of the young people's mothers were in paid—either full-time and part-time—employment outside of the home. Their mothers worked as cleaners, nurses, shop assistants, social workers, local government officers and teachers. Tracey Reynolds (2005) in her study about contemporary Caribbean mothering asserts that paid employment, on top of child rearing and other domestic responsibilities, is a central and longstanding feature of Caribbean mothers collective identity in the U.K.

There were a few mothers (all lone-parents with younger dependant children) who were registered as unemployed but who worked within the informal 'cash-in-hand' economy as cleaners, carers, dressmakers, bar workers and waitresses. Many of these mothers had very little or no formal education and could only secure low-paid menial employment. It was more economically viable for them to continue claiming Housing Benefit and Income Support than it was for them to work and pay tax within the formal economy (see, Watt, 2003).

Whilst the majority of domestic living arrangements within this study corresponded to the lone-female headed household, the nature and quality of family relationships—notably between the young people and their mothers—varied considerably. At least half of my informants described their relationship with their mothers as being very close and nurturing. Griot, a black young male:

> My mom's like my best friend … Yeah we argue and she shouts at me, but I think that now I've got older I can tell my mom a lot of things. I tell my mom like everything, like some things I can't tell her but most things I do tell her. 'Cos it don't really bother me. She knows everything about me, for seventeen years like, so there's no point me hiding.

When I asked Eddie—twenty-one year-old black male—about his heroes, he put forward his mothers name:

> 'Cos no matter what the odds were she was the one who was working three or four shifts a day for three or four different work places. Just because she had to sort of thing, and you know even though we had teenage angst, girl problems, spots and all the rest of it, she was still there for us you know. I don't tell her everyday 'cos it feels funny and I'm a big lad and I'm proud. and obviously I don't want her to start hugging me and the rest of it, but she knows in her own way that she's my hero you know. There's a lot of other people that I respect, but as a heroine it's my mom.

For a lot of Caribbean young men their mothers are of paramount significance and importance, this is illustrated with regard to dissing. Within the peer group the young men like to verbally ridicule each other as a means of entertainment and show-manship. There is an un-spoken rule that members of the group can diss each other about virtually any subject, except those involving an individual's mother. When the rules of engagement are broken in such a manner—disrespecting a young person's mother—it is expected that the wounded party takes vengeance normally in the form of physical violence, in order that he might reclaim the reputation of his mother as well as himself.

One hot summer night during a session at the youth centre the Poppettes[6] were sitting in the centre talking, when the Arms House Crew arrived. On spotting Maria (one of the Poppettes), all of the Arms House[7] boys started goading Nathaniel—one of their members—asking him what he was gonna do about a certain situation. Nathaniel did not seem interested and was smiling trying to drop the subject, but his friends kept goading him until he had to do something. He then called Maria and they disappeared for ten minutes outside of the youth centre. On their return, I noticed Maria had tears in her eyes and her face looked red. I then called her into my office and asked her if she was alright, and tried to find out what had taken place outside with Nathaniel. She said she was alright and that nothing had happened. I then called Nathaniel into the office and he also said nothing had happened. It was only after we had shut the centre that I found out Nathaniel had slapped Maria after an earlier argument they had when she called Nathaniel's mother a bitch in front of his friends. At the time the incident occurred, apparently Nathaniel had been very angry and had said to his mates that he 'ain't having that'. But after the incident it seems he wanted to forget about it, except that his mates would not let him. They were goading him, calling him a 'pussy' and saying, 'how can you let someone disrespect your mom and not do something about it, 'nah you're pussy hole'. The goading had got the better of him. But incidentally Nathaniel, who has a tough no nonsense reputation, took Maria out of view of his peers to do what he allegedly did. Whereas it would have been better for his 'rep' (reputation) if he had done it in front of his peers. I am not that sure that he even hit her, it would not have surprised me if he told Maria to act like as if he had hit her in order that he might save face.

Little Man and Mr. Business further articulate this issue of dissing mothers:

> *Little Man:* and when people diss your mom, it ain't about that. If people yeah, alright but when people go for real, then that's when you're meant to knock people out.
>
> *Mr. Business:* Exactly, 'cos if anyone talks about my mom like that then they're looking to get damaged.

6   The Poppettes are a tight grouping of up to seven young women. They comprise of one young women of African-Caribbean descent, one of mixed Irish/African parentage with the rest being white.

7   Arms House Crew are a loose collective of African-Caribbean young men who live in the nearby Arms House area.

A.G.: What about if someone was to diss your dad, would it be the same?

*Little Man:* Nah, it ain't really.

*Mr. Business:* Yeah, 'cos it's like my dad like. With my mom now, she's a mom you get me, I'm like the baby to my mom you get me.

*Little Man:* I know, I know … I'm my mom's little boy so like, I have to look after my mom. With my dad now, I wouldn't take it as that 'cos he's a man like … Basically if a person cussed my mom I'd take it more personal than if they cuss my dad …

Mr. Business: I'd still do the person some damage though [if they cussed his dad].

*Little Man:* But moms are more important though I think.

A.G.: Why would you say that?

*Little Man:* 'cos I come out of her thingy[8] [both young people start cracking up into fits of laughter].

Whilst half of the young people acknowledged that they had good relationships with their mothers and were able to talk to them freely about most subjects, there was a small minority of young people who only sought to interact with them when they specifically needed to:

*Kanya:* Yeah, I suppose I do get on with her [mother] sometimes, when she's not in one of her moods … I talk to her about things I need to talk to her about, that's it. I ain't got time to be sitting there having like social chats.

Others only communicated with their mothers when they needed money, food or their clothes washed and ironed:

A.G.: How do you get on with your parents, your mom and dad?

*Martin:* With my dad, we always muck about fighting, and my mom she's alright like. I can't explain with my mom because she is … I can't really do much with my mom, my dad I can muck about with, but with my mom I can't, 'cos she's more like feminine and soft, so I can't. I just have to ask her for money and that's it … and ask when's dinner ready.

8 'Thingy' here refers to his mother's vagina.

Of course there was also sizeable minority of young people who did not get on at all with their mothers.

## Parenting in Manor II: Fathers

The academy has tended to ignore the role of black men within the domestic arena, preferring instead to concentrate on their 'alleged' conspicuous displays of aggression, hype-sexuality, and general deviance within public arenas such as on the streets (Liebow, 1967; Pryce, 1979; Majors, 1989). In contradiction to the negative media portrayals of black men as feckless, irresponsible and absentee fathers, Tracey Reynolds, (2001: 151) in her research found that: 'black fathers are active participants in parenting and child care' and that a large proportion of 'fathers who live outside the home assume an [absent present] position, rather than disappearing from the family' altogether. It is important to recognise, as I have argued previously (see chapter one), that all black men are not a homogenous collective of individuals who act, think, speak and dress all in the same way. As such there is very little research evidence that documents the experiences of those black men who, although absent from the family home, do play an active role in their children's lives. Equally it is important to explore the role played by those fathers living at home with their families.

Whilst acknowledging the fact that black men as fathers have been misrepresented as well as under-researched, within this research the role that many fathers—interestingly both black and white—tended to assume within their children's lives was at best peripheral, and at worst non-existent:

A.G.: And how do you get on with your dad?
Eddie: Yeah, my dad's happy with himself and his three litre bottle of coke, you know, just simple things in life for my dad.
A.G.: So do you see much of him?
Eddie: Now and then really. I don't really go round there as much as I should do, but its just that … I don't know … He's changed a lot since I used to go and see him more, so I don't know. I feel he's changed.
A.G.: What about your dad, do you get on with him?
Griot: Yeah, even though I don't see him as much, 'cos I don't live with him, but me and my dad still get on. Occasionally I'll be annoyed … I'll be vexed but like I can never hold it like … Like I love my dad I don't care, life is my dad at the end of the day.
A.G.: Why might you get vexed with your dad?

*Griot:* Maybe if he says he's coming to see us and like he don't turn up
… he's always got a reason so, you fall back on that and say don't worry
about it, there's always another day. It's not like he's not there, 'cos he is
there. Maybe not there when you want him the most, but he's there.
*Tony C:* My old man he lives in … [a nearby neighbourhood] he's got a
separate life, but I see him every week and we talk and that but you know,
it's like a friend relationship between me and my dad. It ain't a father and
son type of relationship, it's more like a mate, I see him … and we're like
mates really so you know that's how it is.

Even though many of these informants didn't see their fathers as much as they
would have liked, at least there was a semblance of some sort of a relationship,
and in some cases a great deal of affection also. Unfortunately, this was not the
case with all of the young people. Mr. Business did not like his father and spent
no time whatsoever with him. There were occasions when Mr. Business's father
would drive past his home and not even bother to drop by and see how he was
doing. Consequently, as far as Mr. Business was concerned since his dad had
no time for him, then he would have no time for his father. Davey, who is black,
recalled how on his twenty-first birthday not even receiving a card, or a telephone
call from his father. I remember walking down the road with Davey, —two or
three years prior to undertaking this research project—when we walked past a
middle aged black man, he casually turned to me and said 'that was my dad who
just walked past us there'. I quickly turned back in disbelief, and asked Davey
why he had not said anything to him. Davey just shrugged his shoulders and
smirked. When I interviewed Maria she nonchalantly remarked: 'I don't really
like my dad, I have seen him a couple of times, like he took me and Jada (her
friend) to Pizza Hut one time, but that was it'.

In addition many of the fathers had second families, which then placed
additional tensions upon already strained relationships with their children.

*Darlene:* yeah my dad's been getting on my nerves lately, because like I
don't see him that much. I don't ask him for that much, well I don't ask
him for anything, but when I do ask him it's for little bits or whatever,
and he can't give it. I just think sometimes that's out of order, 'cos I'm
his only daughter, whether or not Rita [father's partner] has got kids or
not. I'm his only daughter.

*Kanya:* I ain't got a relationship with my dad, he's just sick I swear to God. I don't know he just doesn't do nothing, he's not all there. He rings my house or comes to my house when he feels like it and expects to ask for money. Nah, I don't like him he's a tramp. He gets on my nerves, he's got two other boys yeah that don't live with him, and they're only little and because they moved out, they used to live in ... [South East London] and they moved now all the way to Bristol, and like I ain't got no contact with them. So I asked to get their address, you know so that I could write to them to see if I could get any contact or whatever, and he started coming up with so much crap, any excuse yeah just to say well basically that he's not gonna give us it, 'cos he doesn't want to see them and uh, uh, uh, uh 'cos of the mom and madness. I think I've learnt now not to ask him for anything.

*Sweet Boy:* My dad he lives in ... [town just outside of London] he's just worried about, he's just bothered about, say he's got a little baby girl now, she's about one and his wife.

*A.G.:* Do you see him much?

*Sweet Boy:* No, I haven't seen him for a few months.

The majority of my informants—regardless of their gender and ethnicity—did not feel that their fathers were as actively involved in their lives as perhaps they might have been. Furthermore, a sizable minority of these young people had no contact at all with their fathers. The implications for many young people, of being continually let down and/or rejected by fathers, is rather grave, particularly those vulnerable and/or socially excluded young people. It must be noted that the recent research studies looking at family life in East London (see, Mumford and Power 2003; and Dench et al. 2006) note the increasing marginalised and problematic role of men in family life within poorer neighbourhoods.

## Influence of family and peer group on black young men's transitions

Many writers and academics have attributed the perennial black (male) youth 'problem' to the dysfunctionality of black family life (see chapter one) where there is a dearth of male role models, or elders in the community as allegedly was the case in traditional African societies (Majors, 2000). Whilst black household structures in Britain simply reproduce those family norms found in the Caribbean (Goulbourne and Chamberlain, 2001), many of the support structures that exist in the Caribbean are sadly not present here in Britain; namely the large extended kinship/community networks that might for example provide financial, emotional and child care support to lone-mother households.

Without strong family ties or male role models around to support these young men in their transition(s) to adulthood, so the black masculinities thesis purports, young black males turn to their peer group for that strong sense of familial belonging. In so doing, they run the risk of becoming more deeply embroiled within the hyper-masculine world of black street sub-culture, which serves to pull them further away from the values, mores and institutions of mainstream British society. Within this study, I found that those young men (and women) who did have good and strong relationships with their parents were less likely to get sucked into the world of 'badness' and were more likely to be clear about doing well in school and/or college. Similarly, those young people whom were experiencing difficulties and conflict within their home environment were most at risk from becoming embroiled in the more negative aspects of road culture.

Will was sixteen when I first met him and he was just about to take his GCSEs. He used to live in a middle-class area of East London with his mother—who worked in the city as a legal executive—and his younger brother. Will's father had emigrated back to Jamaica, leaving his family behind. Since Will's father had left, Will's relationship with his mother had deteriorated rapidly. Will had had a very good relationship with his father who instilled in him the values of working hard and doing well at school. Whilst Will was still doing well at school he started to hang about with a gang of white young men who lived in his area, it was at this point that Will was introduced to life 'on road'. Just before Will's sixteenth birthday his mother threw him out of the family home after one too many arguments and disagreements. Will's father, from his new home in Jamaica, was able to sort out for Will to stay at his Godfather's house in Manor. Will managed to pass seven G.C.S.Es at grade A-C and enrolled at a nearby sixth form college whilst working part-time at Tescos. Also at this point, I was able to refer him to be housed at a nearby Foyer housing project for young people. In the Foyer project Will got more and more embroiled in 'road culture', eventually dropping out of college and making a living from selling drugs and partaking in numerous 'scams'[9]. Will acknowledged that although he was aware

---

9   'Scams' here refer to illegal money making ventures involving obtaining expensive goods via stolen credit cards etc.

that his environment was dragging him down, the pull of his peers was at times too strong to resist.

Twenty-three year old d.j. Wildstyle, who is of African-Caribbean descent, articulates well the attraction of the peer group:

> *Wildstyle*: What I've found is that you totally identify through the street culture thing, its like if you've got a nickname your known as that person … if your someone to know your someone and that's what its all bout, image and identity that's what everything for us revolved around being on the street … and if you had a strong identity within that then you were somebody, that was your life.
> *A.G.*: What did you do on the street?
> *Wildstyle*: Drink, smoke cause trouble, basically do things that you couldn't do at home, which is most things.

Interestingly Wildstyle also connects the young people's involvement with road culture to their family connections, or lack of them.

> *Wildstyle*: Why I said it was a strong sense of identity on the streets was because, if you got in trouble in school you didn't care, if you did anything outside the area [neighbourhood] you didn't care, but say you had an argument amongst your mates, and I can remember times when I was younger, where I had an argument with someone, and what happened is a lot of people took the side of the other person and like you didn't go out for a couple days, and that was like your whole world was come apart. Also I just think family ties made what you did on the streets slightly different to what some of the others might did. It's like we all used to do madness[10], but there was always a limit for me, compared to say some of the others who like had no boundaries as far as like what they were prepared to do … I knew what would happen to me at home if I went beyond a certain point. Whereas without making generalisations, like with some of the other kids, where maybe they didn't have strong family ties or what have you, they would do anything [on road] … One time I got caught smoking 'cos they [his parents] was very observant of me, like I'd come in smelling of cigarettes you know what I mean.
> *A.G.*: And what happened to you?

10 Madness here is referring to 'badness' like petty crime, fighting and smoking and/or selling

*Wildstyle:* I got grounded … and that's when I started to realise who my true friends were, 'cos I can remember being grounded and not many people knocked for me and that hurt, it really cut me … really really cut … 'cos them times now, your mates were like your whole world and that.

Wildstyle lived at home with both his parents and readily admitted that at the time he believed them to be too strict—in comparison to his friends' parents— but that it served him in good stead for later life, and he now appreciates what they did for him. Also he felt that those of his peers who did get sucked into a career of 'badness' did so to rebel against their parents, and maybe they felt did not care about them enough:

*Wildstyle:* At the time I thought my parents was way too strict and I didn't like it. But I can appreciate it now, because of the way I've turned out. But when I was a kid growing up all my friends could go and play around the back [of the estate], I couldn't play round the back, if I wasn't in the sight of my parents I couldn't play, and its like when it was time to come in, when all the other kids were out till like eleven [p.m.] I was in at six or seven [p.m.], you know what I mean and, I had to sit and watch through the window whilst my friends played out but I couldn't go out there, and if I begged to go out there I'd get beats for it you know, and it was strict the upbringing was strict, but I think it was a good type of strict now, but at the time I resented it.

*Charley:* Because it put you on the straight and narrow you haven't never been in prison, you've not really done bad, bad … I mean you've done badness but not like, you haven't took like an excessive amount of drugs like as in hard drugs.

*Wildstyle:* I think in a sense as well, I think with a lot of drugs taken by young people it's unhappiness.

*Charley:* I do, that's exactly what I did.

*Wildstyle:* Even though I resented the strictness I was still reasonably happy. I had all the love I needed you know what I mean, I had everything so at the end of the day I didn't need to be rebellious, I didn't feel the need to get at my parents, a lot of what I did was peer pressure, you know what I mean, we're going to nick this … your in it your inside of it, you can't lose face, my image was important and it (image) was a good one. At the time I couldn't, the thought of saying 'no I don't wanna do that', was just not a thought, it just couldn't be done, do you know what I mean. I had to do it, but I never had no desire to get back at my parents to make them notice me 'cos I was very much noticed.

Of course there were many parents who tried hard to keep their male children away from the more negative aspects of the 'road culture', but through no fault of their own seemed to be waging a losing battle: When I first met Raymond (at the age of twelve) he was a very quiet and unassuming young man, but during the subsequent years he was to grow much taller as well more confident and rebellious. He was not the type of character who would cross the road to avoid a fight. At one point I (along with his mother who is a nurse) became rather concerned as he seemed to be getting more and more embroiled within the more negative aspects of the 'road culture'. He started to take to hanging about the streets 'tooled up'[11], getting into fights and 'jacking' people (robbing people with violence). He was permanently excluded from one school and refused admittance to his local school because of his bad record. His mother managed to fight for him to be diagnosed as dyslexic, but right up to when he had left secondary school he did not get any support with it. Even in his new school there were certain teachers who said he was a violent menace who should be permanently excluded from their school. On one particular occasion his mother rang my mobile phone at her wits end, as he had been arrested. She asked me if I could have a word with him, as he was much bigger than her and did not seem to listen to her or take her very seriously any more. As a man whom he liked and got along well with, she believed I might be able to get through to him. I always found Raymond to be a respectful and pleasant young man, but he was just getting too enmeshed in the world of 'badness'. His mother worked hard and fought for him within the education system, but his dyslexia was never picked up and dealt with effectively.

---

11  Tooled up refers to a weapon, either a knife, baseball bat or heavy blunt instrument.

**Chapter Six**

# Road culture I: Life on road

This chapter seeks neither to valorise[1] nor problematise[2] black British youth subcultures, but rather attempts to illustrate the seductive yet humdrum and functional role—as opposed to the 'spectacular' which has characterised a good deal of subcultural research (Gelder, 1997)—of 'road subculture' in the day-to-day lives of the majority of young people in this study. I specifically adopt this methodological perspective because:

> The social texture of everyday human humdrum activity is a major aspect of or component of any enduring social ambience, and the description of such texture allows the more dramatic events to which anthropologists usually attend to be located against a backdrop which gives them shape.
>
> (Lieber, 1976: 321)

Here, I will attempt to ascertain the influence of road culture on the lives of the young people—particularly the way in which the informants derive camaraderie, entertainment, as well as a strong sense of identity and belonging—during the phase in their lives when they are experiencing rapid physical, emotional, and psychological change.

## Road cultures in East London

Within this study road subculture is viewed as a continuum, where occupying the centre ground are the vast majority of nondescript 'boring' young people, with a small minority of young men—who immerse themselves into the world of 'badness'[3]—taking up the extreme margins (see chapter eight). Of course there are a small number of young men who continually travel back and forth between the centre and the margins of the subculture. In essence road culture is not about the margins at all, its life force is derived from the majority of young people who make up its centre ground. In this chapter, my interest in

1   See Gilroy, 1987a and 1993a; Hebdige, 1987; Jones, 1991; Alexander, 1996; Back, 1996.
2   See Patterson, 1965; Cashmore, 1979; Pryce, 1979; Cashmore and Troyna, 1982; Sewell, 1997.
3   'Badness' refers to a social world characterised by 'spectacular' hyper aggressive/hyper masculine modes of behaviour, usually centreing around violent/ petty crime and low level drug-dealing

road culture stems mainly from a concern with how, where, and with whom the young people spend the majority of their leisure time, as well exploring some of the reasoning behind these leisure choices.

Road culture in Manor and the surrounding neighbourhoods—as is the case with wider black and mainstream British road youth cultures—is largely influenced by expressive black diasporic popular cultures (Gilroy, 1987a and 1993a). Nevertheless, I would hesitate to define or portray road culture in exclusively racial/ethnic terms, as this 'black' reading fails to recognise the participation of large numbers of white and other minority ethnic working-class youth. Furthermore, the House/Rave musical soundtracks of Jungle, Drum 'n' Bass, and UK Garage[4]—which also inspire road life in Manor—are themselves hybrid forms (see Reynolds, 1998; Bidder, 2001) that could only have been created within Britain via its many deprived and run down multi ethnic urban/suburban tower blocks and council housing estates. With regard to white participation in the jungle subcultural scene of the early 1990s Reynolds (1998) argues that:

> Even Nation of Islam influenced militants like Kemet Crew stress that jungle has always been a black-and-white scene … Jungle is a kick in the eye for both white power organisations like the BNP and for black segregationists, because it shows that trans-racial alliances are possible. Not just because it make 'blackness' seem cool to white kids, but because there's a genuine unity of experience shared by Britain's black and white underclass.                                                    (ibid.: 248)

According to Reynolds this common unity of experience shared by the black and white underclass is about:

> inhabiting the same run-down tower blocks and council estates, being harassed by the police, living for marijuana, break beats and b-b-b-bass … Even when they live in nowheresville suburbs like Hitchin and Romford rather than inner-city ghettos, junglists belong to the jilted generation who are bored and frustrated, and have little to live for but burning up dead time in a weekend's full of jungle fever.                          (ibid.: 248)

---

4   UK Garage refers to a variety of sub genres including Grime, 2-Step, and Bass-Line.

Finally—as well as more controversially, for Reynolds, 'junglist is defined not by race, but by class, in so far as all working-class urban youth are 'niggas', in the eyes of authority' (ibid.: 248).

Reynolds' observations about white youth participation and trans-racial friendships/alliances within the jungle scene—although romanticised on one level[5]—born out of a commonality of experience between black and white working-class young people, can equally be applied to the UK Garage influenced 'road cultures' of Manor and the surrounding neighbourhoods. As to whether road culture is in fact a black youth subculture, Charley, a twenty-one year old young white female has this to say about feeling more comfortable around black people than white people:

> I mean what is culture that's what I say, what is it? You're saying because you're black you have to hold onto certain things and you have to be a certain way. No, I think its how you feel, if you feel comfortable on one side of things [either with majority of black people or a majority of white people] then go there and feel comfortable, there's no point trying to fit somewhere where you don't feel comfortable, yeah I think they miss out [other white racist individuals who might criticise her for having too many black friends and being too heavily involved in road cultural life], they miss out on the music, they miss out on the culture, I can't even say culture because I can't say it's a black culture, I'd say there's a street culture and they [racist whites] miss out on that, because I would say that more black people take up the street culture.

As hinted at by Charley in the above statement, within Manor and the surrounding districts there are clear distinctions between black influenced road culture and Grafter culture. The Grafter youth subculture draws specifically on white working class East End traditions, but again there are a number of black youth who actively participate within this scene alongside their white peers. Consequently, each group is not hermetically sealed of from, or antagonistic toward the other—indeed movement between the two is both fluid and commonplace due to interracial friendships and alliances:

---

5    There is definitely a commonality of experience between black and white working-class youth in Manor, yet
     it would be wrong to overstress the significance and importance of class and spatial location at the expense
     of race/ethnicity. Black young people in Manor still have different experiences from their white

*dj Wildstyle:* Even now with like my white friends, even though they're in with us [road culture] they've still got that different thing going on, like you go to work, come home with the newspaper in the back pocket, rolled up in your back pocket, go to the pub straight after work in your work clothes. It's never like an office job or a job that requires a certain amount of knowledge … it's painting and decorating.

*David:* It's like, I'm going Graftin ennit?

*dj Wildstyle:* That is the term, grafters, they're grafters hence we work on the roads, we do electrical installation, we paint and decorate, we do roofing, come home go to the pub, get up at six in the morning and go back to work, in the pub all weekend, eat the Sunday roast.

The differences in lifestyle and outlook (as illustrated by dj Wildstyle) between those male informants involved within the Grafter and road subcultures, becomes even more distinct when the young people turn sixteen and leave school. At this point the Grafters will usually find non skilled or semi skilled positions within the building or construction industries, with the pub taking over from the roads and youth centre as the focal point where they spend the majority of their leisure time. On the other hand, when those young men involved in road culture turn sixteen they will usually enrol at a local college (or at least sporadically turn up for lectures), obtain part-time or casual employment within the clean and non-manual service sector, or else become more heavily involved in the more negative aspects of road life. For these young men involved in road culture, the streets (UK Garage, R'n'B and Jamaican Bashment) are still the main focal point for the majority of their leisure time activities.

## Our neighbourhood

Postmodernist discourses on 'place'—or a 'given social space with a clearly demarcated, historically rooted, cultural signification'. (Watt, 1998: 691)—have tended to be tied up with those debates around globalisation and the wider politics of 'identification'. Here, it is argued that the globalised political economy (Lash and Urry, 1994; Waters, 1995) with its emphasis on the flexible accumulation of capital and subcontracting has resulted in the destruction of traditional local labour markets and community life. Also the growth in mass communications and the media has meant that many individuals now derive their social and cultural meanings, not from the local neighbourhood, but from the globalised media comprising of the internet, television and cinema. As such the post-modern take on city localities is that they have become 'no-place' spaces (Featherstone, 1991: 99) that have become increasingly insignificant within young people's lives.

On the other hand, critics have pointed out that much of these debates on 'place' and identity have been largely theoretical in nature. There has been very little in the way of a grounded empirical analysis that might illuminate the complexity of contemporary place identities' (May, 1996). However, during the past twenty years there have been a number of empirically grounded studies of young people that have contradicted the postmodernist arguments concerning the decreasing importance of 'place'. Alexander (1996), in her study of black youth illustrated how strong local identities existed, that were also linked to essentialised notions of black identity. Furthermore, a number of other recent ethnographic youth studies[6] have also shown that young people still exhibit strong attachments to their local neighbourhoods.

All of the young people featured in this study attached a great deal of importance to their local neighbourhood, exhibiting strong 'place' identities. Manor had featured in the news-media (both local and national) quite a lot during the past few years as a number of murders (stabbings and shootings) had taken place locally. For many young people this showed that Manor was a place of great significance due to its national notoriety. On one particular occasion Sweet Boy and Raymond were in the games room of the youth club talking proudly about Manor. Raymond was bragging about how Manor is one of the most roughest and violent areas in England, as there had been ''nuff shootings and killings round here' recently. In a previous conversation with Helen (a black teacher who worked in a local secondary school and who had grown up in an adjoining neighbourhood) she had told me how when she was growing up her older brothers never liked going to clubs and pubs in Manor because of the fear of getting stabbed or beaten up; it had a rough reputation even twenty years ago. Raymond in particular seemed to like the fact that Manor had a rough reputation, as he was swaggering about the room confidently, re-telling the story to any one that would listen to him.

The notoriety of the area was proudly upheld by the younger generations who, as in the case of the Arms House Crew, looked to step out of the shadows of their older peers by doing 'badness' in order to get a 'rep'[7] for themselves. As viewed from their own perspective, the Arms House young men have a reputation to

6   See Westwood, 1990; Callaghan, 1992; Pearce, 1996; Taylor et al., 1996; Webster, 1996; O'Byrne, 1997; Watt and Stenson, 1998; Back et al., 1999; Nayak, 2003; Shildrick, 2006.

7   'Rep' or 'reputation'-getting kudos from being known as someone who was into 'badness' and was tough and street-smart.

uphold that was handed down to them from an earlier generation. This acute 'localism' is also identified in the studies of Parker, (1974) and Patrick, (1973), where the 'street corner milieu' demands that the Arms House torch be carried on in the future. One outcome of the aggressive 'maverick masculinities' adopted by the Arms House Crew is that any vulnerable young person is at risk from getting 'jacked' or beaten up:

A.G.: So what do you really think about Arms Crew and that lot?

*Lazy Boy*: I don't think they're as rough as they make out, it's all mouth with them I think.

A.G.: 'cos Grafters and them don't get on do they, they don't fight but it's like?

*Lazy Boy*: Nah, we're alright with them, but we don't like, if we're walking down the street we won't, we'll stop and talk to them, but we won't mix or hang about with them, because they're trouble makers that's why, they like making trouble.

A.G.: What kind of things do they do?

*Lazy Boy*: Like they can walk down the street and see someone and they start calling him names and all that, so that's not us.

A.G.: What about fighting … do they rob people as well?

*Lazy Boy*: Well bwoy, I wouldn't like to say.

A.G.: Why do you think they are the way they are?

*Lazy Boy:* I think what it is, is they're following the older lot, I think they're following them.

A.G.: What did they used to do?

*Lazy Boy:* Whatever ennit?

A.G.: But you knew of them?

Lazy Boy: Yeah, I knew of them.

A.G.: 'cos the older Grafters lot were rough as well ennit?

*Lazy Boy:* Yeah, they was rougher, in the Grafters [Estate] they used to have signs saying enter at your own risk.

A.G.: So what's happened to all them lot now?

*Lazy Boy:* As they got older they like got more mature.

## Badness and road culture

For the majority of young black males in Manor, road life is not about badness but rather it is centred upon meeting up with friends, 'hanging on road', attending the youth club, raving, looking 'links' and 'catching joke'. In essence road life is about friendships, routine and the familiar as well as 'doing nothing' (Corrigan, 1979).

Jamaica and the United states are the principal external cultural driving forces of East London (and British) youth subculture(s) via the speech styles, dress wear and attitudes associated with the black popular music forms of Bashment and Hip-Hop. Both these musical forms have successfully managed to convey, through song lyrics, the significance and general acceptance of 'badness-honour'—which according to Obika Gray is an oral kinetic practice in Jamaica which employs a repertoire of violent and intimidating language, physical gestures and actions that 'enables claimants, usually from disadvantaged groups, to secure ... a modicum of power and respect' (Gray, 2003: 18)—and the perennial appeal of the 'bad ass', the 'bad nigger' and the 'rude boy' within the ghettos and poor neighbourhoods of Jamaica and black-America (see Gray, 2003; Van Deburg, 2004). The cool and hip image of the black outlaw within black popular culture holds a strong appeal amongst a small number of the young black males who lived in Manor and 'practiced badness'—within this study I refer to these young males as 'rude boys'. For the small number of young men who practiced badness being a criminal was viewed negatively and there was no kudos or value attached to such a term. In contrast however, a rude boy or 'ghetto don' is about power, as it entails having the entire neighbourhood fear you, 'look up to you' or 'aspire to be like you'.

The road cultural style and fashion (as adopted by the majority of black male youth) is very much influenced by the hyper-masculine and style conscious attitudes and personas of the 'rude boys'. Therefore, the majority of young males involved in road life will tend to walk around in small groups, wearing designer sportswear (Nike sportswear is the brand of choice followed by Addidas and then Reebok) hooded sports tops and jackets (normally with hood up, even in blazing sunshine), baseball caps, tracksuit bottoms or straight legged designer trousers or denim jeans. To get the straight legged effect, the trousers or jeans are taken in from just below the knee right down to the ankles to give drain pipe effect. Designer labels of choice for trousers, jeans and shirts are Versace, Valentinos, Stone Island, Iceberg, Armani and Moschino. When walking these young black males will look to 'hog the pavement' (thus making it difficult for other members of the public to pass by without having to step into the road) by walking in small groups oblivious to other pavement users needs. They also will adopt a 'screw face' (described at best as a blank expression, at worst as hostile and aggressive) in order to warn potential male foes that they are 'not to be messed with'. In short these young males are putting out a message that they are not victims (weak or 'pussies') rather they are the victimisers.

Unfortunately, to the outside world these young males (majority of black male youth) are indistinguishable from 'rude boys'—small minority black male youth—as illustrated by journalists such as Tim Lott:

> My chief prejudice seems to focus on young black males whom I presume to be West Indian—specifically those who wear hooded tops in hot weather, ride very small bikes much too fast and hang around in large groups on the streets ... It mainly arises from the vague suspicion that they are inconsolably grumpy, somewhat misogynist and contemptuous of the law and of white society in general ... Such feelings are the dirty little secret of many, if not most, white liberals ....
>
> (*London Evening Standard*, 27 June 2002)

It is not only 'white liberals' and journalists who feel anger and hostility toward today's generation of urban black (particularly male) youth, there are a number of mainly older black individuals whose viewpoints are not too dissimilar to those of Tim Lott:

> *Richie:* At the end of the day I'm a black man, I grew up through it. I know what its like out there on road. I mean, how I am now to how I was back then is a totally different thing, 'cos I was a ragamuffin but in a totally different way. The problem I'm finding now though, is the way how some of these young black boys go on nowadays, they cannot go in their homes and speak and act how they do. When they come out on the streets they take on this attitude, and sometimes I stand there and it just disgusts me. I'll be standing on Priory Lane where my dad works in a shop and we'll see a white boy walk in, he'll say please and thank you very much. What I find is when white people grow up they can cuss and swear in their house. They go and come and as they please, they [white kids] are the most unruly children at home ever. These young black boys have

got the strict upbringing, but they go in the shop [gimme da ting man]. I stand there and I look, and I look like this [showing facial expression) and I think to myself [It's disgraceful], understand what I'm saying. They've go no respect for things, for nothing. They've got no respect outside of their home. ... When I see these young boys going on with that attitude it disgusts me because we have stereotypes enough as it is in society, and you don't need to add to it. That's my opinion anyway.

(black male, part-time youth worker, aged 25)

Of course there are a good number of young men as described by Richie and Tim Lott who feel slighted at being wrongly stereotyped as being rude, aggressive and truculent:

*Griot:* Like you can see us on the [street] corner and you think they're talking about mugging someone, but we're talking about business or we're talking about college, what we're doing at college and what job we're gonna have and that. So people just don't know, you have to take time to look at a person in depth to find out what they're really like, and that's what a lot of people don't do. They just make assumptions toward you, and just say yeah [that's what you are], 'cos your that colour [black] or your doing that. It's like if someone saw me on the street corner and I had my hood up, like jogging bottoms on or whatever and I'm standing there, obviously they think [oh what's he doing, he's probably gonna mug someone or he's doing drugs]. But it's only what they see, they just see me [tall young black male] they just see my clothes, and they get the wrong idea. So really they have to come up and actually talk to me, then actually find out how wrong they were.

Such stereotypes and negative perceptions are not necessarily restricted to black male youth, their female counterparts also experience hostility too:

*Darlene:* They would be scared [white people], but they're scared anyway. 'cos they hear about black people do this and black people do that, and black people mug this one.
*Kanya:* Just stereotyping ennit?
*Darlene:* Yeah, and they do this and they do that, but I think what people need to understand is that everyone's just different.

*Kanya:* Even Sandra, remember Sandra what she said? She was walking going to school and some old lady was coming off the train and she had her bag like this [visually demonstrates], and her hand bag, when she saw Sandra you should have seen how quickly she grabbed it, and then Sandra thought it was actually quite rude, she wasn't gonna do anything.
*Darlene:* I would get upset if that happened to me.
*Kanya:* I would as well.
*Darlene:* I mean that's just upsetting.

Many young black males involved in road culture feel compelled to adopt and take on 'rude boy' aesthetics and posturing, as a means of negotiating their own 'safe' path through the potential dangers of hyper-masculinist neighbourhood life. Stolzoff, (2000) in his ethnographic study of Jamaican Dance Hall culture describes how young males from the:

> White Hall Crew (ghetto area of Kingston, Jamaica) tended to romanticise those who were victimisers rather than victims. Ricky Trooper told me [you can't make a man kill you.] Being an innocent victim is one of the deepest fears of a ghetto youth man.
>
> (Stolzoff, 2000: 138)

Likewise black male youth in Manor preferred to ally themselves with the perceived neighbourhood 'winners' (rude boys) as opposed to its 'losers' (pussies and chiefs[8]), whilst at the same time privately condemning, and keeping at a safe (but friendly) distance from those 'rude boys' who they are not related to, or 'tight'[9] with. When a group of rude boys from Manor 'rush'[10] or 'jack' an unknown (a young person either from Manor or a surrounding neighbourhood with no obvious familial or peer group attachments[11]), most young men in public will just shrug their shoulders as if to say 'well that's just how things are on road', whereas in private they will acknowledge that those (Manor rude boys) who did it were 'out of order', they shouldn't have picked on an innocent. Yet street logic—or the code of street (see Anderson, 1999)—dictates that sympathy for

---

8   A chief is a simpleton, an idiot who can be easily taken advantage of (bullied and robbed) by their more street smart peers.
9   'Tight' refers to close friendships and alliances.
10  Rush, where a group of young men violently assault a smaller group (or an individual) of young men.
11  Such attachments are essential for young people in terms of back up and the possible retribution for an act of bullying, violence and robbery.

the victim is at best fleeting and generally non-sympathetic as 'they (victim) shouldn't have allowed themselves to be chiefed off like that', because there is no way that they 'would allow themselves to be mugged off like that by no one'. On the other hand when the Manor 'rude boys', 'jack' or 'rush' a 'known'[12] but disliked young person (possibly a 'rude boy' who has been going on stink'[13], or a young male with a god 'rep' and strong familial or peer group attachments), street logic determines that the 'chief' probably got what he deserved as he was beginning to believe too much 'in his own hype', running about upsetting 'too many of the man them' in the neighbourhood.

## Public spaces I: Hanging out on road

Road culture in Manor (and the surrounding neighbourhoods) is played out predominantly within the public sphere, with young people choosing to spend the majority of their leisure time on the streets or within those open spaces to be found around the various local housing estates[14]. Youth clubs, night clubs (or Raves), cinemas, and to a much lesser extent the local shopping malls were also popular hanging out sites for the youth of Manor. The term 'road' as opposed to street culture is referred to throughout this study in recognition of the young people's own definition of their subculture as 'being on road' or as 'living on road'. There is a subtle distinction between the two latter statements, whereas the majority of young people might talk of 'being on road' and 'catching joke'[15] with their friends or looking to make 'links'[16], it is only those young people involved in 'badness' who are referred to as 'living on road'. Whilst the majority of the young people can be viewed as voracious but judicious consumers of road cultural life, for a small minority of young men 'life on road' is everything and consumes most aspects of their day-to-day lives.

---

12  A known young person is someone who is not necessarily a 'rude boy', but has a reputation either as someone who can physically look after themselves (through fighting) or has good 'back up' via familial or peer group attachments. There are also young men who are 'known' and respected (and generally well liked) maybe because they're funny, good at sports or music (particularly dj-ing, mc-ing).

13  Stink here denotes those 'rude boys' who refuse to play by the rules as determined within the world of 'badness', so maybe they are 'jacking' young people indiscriminately and therefore creating lot of potential enemies within the neighbourhood.

14  For similar observations see, Wilmott, 1966; Patrick, 1973; Parker, 1974; Corrigan, 1979; McLeod, 1987; Anderson, 1990, Anderson, 1999; Alexander, 1996; Back, 1996; Watt and Stenson, 1998; Robson, 2000.

15  'Catching joke' is where young people relay humorous stories and situations back to each other, talk about girls or boys and generally 'diss' (name calling/mickey taking) each other.

16  'Links' or 'link ups', sexual liaisons between young men and young women—more than just friends but less than girl/boyfriends.

Lieber (1976: 319) argues that the '[hanging around] characteristic of those involved in urban street scenes must be interpreted as work and as activity', 'hanging about on road' is not essentially about 'doing nothing' (see, Corrigan, 1979).

> *Griot*: Erm, what do I do in my spare time? Erm, sometimes I hang about on street corners where we'll all like meet up and chat on street, or we play football, basketball, go out raving. I can say that us in Manor, we do things, we do creative things with our time, we never really loaf[17], we don't loaf around. If we're on road we're like doing something constructive, we're not causing trouble, we don't really cause no serious trouble we just like to have a laugh.

Road life is also about identity and belonging where according to dj Wildstyle it becomes:

> A way of living, a way of viewing things. It's like a viewpoint, the way you look at life sort of thing. You speak a certain way, even with the street talk, it's like your speaking another language. I mean if you're not from around here you wouldn't have a clue what we were talking about, it's definitely about having a sense of identity. What I've found is that you totally identify through the street culture thing, its like if you've got a nickname, then your known as that person. If you're someone to know, then you are someone [gaining the respect of your peers] and basically that's what its all bout, image and identity. That's what I think personally. In a sense it's a good thing for young people. I mean what else did you do? Everything for us revolved around being on the street, and if you had a strong identity within that [the streets], then you were somebody that was your life (dj Wildstyle).
> A.G.: What did you do on the street?
> *dj Wildstyle*: Basically, we'd do things that you couldn't do at home. So we'd be on the street drinking, smoking [weed/marijuana and cigarettes], laughing, everything, like joking messing around. And like when girls used to pass by us it would be like 'come over here' sort of thing.

---

17  'Loafing' is where young people might hang about with no aim or purpose, they are just killing time.

Not all of the young people viewed 'hanging around' the streets in a positive light and would try to resist from becoming involved. Nonetheless the seduction and appeal of the road would normally prove too much even for them:

> *Darlene:* I'm sick of hanging about on streets now, nah I am 'cos its like I'll come out and where going somewhere, but we'll end up standing on the street, and like a couple of times I've just thought nah I'm not doing this, I wanna get on with what I'm doing, so I just stand there and think what am I doing, I'm standing on street corners chatting to people that ain't gonna get me nowhere, like all them Latymer [neighbourhood bordering Manor] people [all young black men] they ain't gonna get me nowhere.
> A.G.: So you just stand there talking to them?
> *Darlene:* Yeah, and just catch joke and that.

Whereas Griot specifically maintained that 'hanging about' did not entail loafing, his friend Sweet Boy who was more disdainful described it as:

> Just standing there doing nothing, just loafing, that's known as loafing just standing around on road, just talking, just outside say Griot's block, just standing there and talking, sitting on the wall and doing nothing, its called loafing (Sweet Boy).
> A.G.: What might you normally talk about?
> *Sweet Boy:* Nothing, just what's happening … girls, yeah just catch joke.
> A.G.: What, day in day out?
> *Sweet Boy:* Yeah, girls, whatever. Day in day out. That's what we used to do man.

For those young people involved in 'hanging about on road', the pleasure and entertainment value of such activity is mainly derived from meeting up with their friends and 'catching joke' or trying to get 'links', and this was the case regardless of gender:

> *Kanya:* Like in the summer I'll probably come here [youth club], 'cos like they've got like loads of things going on, like all them trips and that. And at other times, just might be on road catching joke, you can't be too serious all the time.
> A.G.: So what is catching joke?

*Darlene:* Standing with man and just laughing about crap.

*Kanya:* If there's loads of us yeah all standing together, whole heap of boys and whole heap of girls yeah, whatever. Just all together, catching joke, doing nothing.

*A.G.:* Do you go out with the boys? [are they boyfriend and girlfriend?]

*Kanya:* Nah.

*Darlene:* There just good friends of ours.

*Kanya:* Yeah they're just good friends of ours we don't do anything with them, they're dumb.

*Darlene:* Exactly, they're dumb but they're friends of ours.

*Kanya:* They're dumb, but if you're like in a stupid mood or whatever you can always like get a joke.

*Darlene:* They're just people we can laugh at.

*Kanya:* Yeah.

*Darlene:* Like, they just stand there and just bus joke [make each other laugh] and certain little things that you will see them doing, you can just laugh at, 'cos they're so stupid.

*Kanya:* It's hard to explain but it's just catching joke basically.

During the winter months many of the young people spent less time 'hanging around' on the streets, preferring instead to meet up with their friends at the youth centre(s), or at Raves/clubs, as well as in the more private domain of each others homes. This latter observation about the higher incidence of home centred leisure activities during the winter months, was particularly true in the case of many of the female informants who mixed 'n' matched masculinist road culture with their own 'bedroom cultures' (see studies by Griffiths, 1988; Pearce, 1996; McNamee, 1998).

*A.G.:* So what do you do when you go around to each other's houses?

*Melinda:* I go to Ayesha's to have something to eat, 'cos I like her mom's cooking [Caribbean food]. Watch telly and ring people.

*Ayesha:* Listen to music.

*Melinda:* Listen to music, sometimes we just walk about and see what we can see sometimes.

*Ayesha:* Most of the time we go to Gerry's [female friend] and like do the same thing, and more people will come round.

*Melinda:* Talk about boys mostly ennit?

Ayesha: Yeah talk about boys, our problems. Like all of us will try and help each other out with our problems.

Of course this did not necessarily mean that there were no groups of young women 'hanging about' the streets in the winter:

A.G.: Hanging about on road, would you say it's mainly a guy thing, whereas perhaps girls might prefer to go round to each other's houses?
*Melinda:* Nah, it's girls as well. Some girls will go out and walk about for hours just doing nothing. Like there are girls who go out, and walk about for hours in the cold, people love to go out in the winter as well don't they? When it's freezing and you just don't see no boys or nothing, they don't care.
*Ayesha:* Yeah, hoping you see people.
*Melinda:* Yeah, if you see people good, like you have jokes and that, when you don't.

## Public spaces II: The sports cage

The youth club in Manor was situated within a small green open space—which was the one green area available amidst the many housing estates, builders yards, warehouses and small factories—and adjoined onto a small children's playground as well as a floodlit caged (iron meshing which enclosed the tarmac and rose to about twelve foot high) outdoor area which served as a five-a-side football pitch and mini basketball court. During most weeknights (in term time) the sports cage was a hive of activity where from about three p.m. each afternoon, small groups of young men would play one-on-one basketball before being overrun (at about six p.m.) by larger groups of young men who would reclaim the space as a football pitch. During the summer months the sports cage would be occupied (from early in morning during school holidays) by large groups of young men right up until eleven p.m. or as soon as it became dark. In the winter months the floodlight would come on (through a timer) at about four p.m. and would not be switched off until well after eleven p.m. that night. Even during the winter period when the nights were cold and dark there would always be large groups of young men playing football or basketball in the cage.

The cage, even though it was in dire need of refurbishment, was integral to road life in Manor as it served as a space where young men could let off steam.

More significantly, the cage offered many young people (particularly males) the opportunity to form new friendships and extend their social networks:

> *Griot:* Before I moved to Manor I hardly knew anyone, but where I've been living here now for seven years, I know loads of people now. There's a lot of friendly people in Manor, its just finding them. 'cos a lot of people out there, they only wanna make a friend they don't wanna cause trouble or nothing. I met quite a lot of people like on the basketball court just from passing by [sports cage], just walking by. And then little after that people start to know your face, and then it's like 'come let we play basketball' so that was a good way of meeting people. I met loads of people like that, you need a meeting place where everyone can just come down and do something constructive. 'Cos with the basketball court, which I want to be refurbished, people are in there from early morning to late at night, and there are never any problems. Like you can just come down and everybody's friendly, you can play with anyone's ball, 'cos at the end of the day your just there to have fun. I think that's one of the best ways the kids in Manor can learn to communicate just by having fun, and that's something that the council or whatever social services need to pick up on. I find that if you give the kids better places to meet up, and like hang out then it will keep 'em off the street, people will be more friendly towards each other, but like I said it's up to them [the local borough Council]. All we can do is talk, 'cos we don't have the money or the resources like, so we leave it up to the borough, to do what they have to do [Griot has been trying to get the Council to refurbish the cage and for them to put new basketball rings up].

The young women of Manor never used the cage, they were more likely to sit on the swings in the small children's playground, chatting to each other or to the boys through the metal fencing (of the adjoining cage) as they played football or basketball. As older groupings, neither the Grafters (who now spent the majority of their leisure time in the pub) nor the Arms House Crew (too heavily embroiled in 'badness' to have time to be running around playing games) used the cage, whereas members of the Pups were always to be found in there.

## Public spaces III: The youth centre

The youth club operated three nights a week and was part of the newly built Manor Children and Young People's Resource facility which operated a varied programme of activities for toddlers, children, and young people. Youth club regulars included members of the Pups, Poppettes, R'n'B Girls, and the Arms House Crew (who despite their age and 'bad boy' reputations still enjoyed hanging out there). For many of the informants the youth club was an extension of road life and served as a warm (particularly in the winter) and safe environment in which to 'pass through'[18], and meet friends, or 'hang out' and 'kotch'[19], 'catch joke' and make 'links':

> A.G.: So tell me more about hanging on road and chasin' man [links]?
> Ayesha: We used to be on the streets like, voice ring[20] 'em 'like are you coming to links us'? [to the Arms House boys]. Then they used to come and then we would be standing on the street corner.
> Melinda: We used to come here [youth club].
> Ayesha: Yeah it was come youth club, like people used to be smoking, doing whatever.
> A.G.: Smoking weed? [marijuana]
> Melinda: Yeah, and the boys [Arms House crew] used to be trying to molest us, and you know us [to me] we would be like 'no', but you know how we was really. Really, we was like do it more, egging 'em on but ...
> A.G.: What to molest you?
> Ayesha: Yeah, we don't mean molest us [laughing] but...
> A.G.: Just give you attention?
> Melinda: Yeah.
> Ayesha: Yeah.
> A.G.: So you liked it really?
> Ayesha: When they're giving us attention, but not too much, like when they go to a certain level, it's like 'stop that'.

18  To 'pass through', here the young person concerned is not looking to 'hang out', they have just briefly stopped by maybe to see someone or pick something up (money, a message, clothes, phones etc.), before going on their way again.

19  To 'kotch' is to sit down and relax/ stay in one place as opposed to 'passing through' or being 'on a mission' where the young person concerned is busy and on the move—because perhaps they have places to go or other people to see.

20  'Voice ring', via mobile phone network, young people dial directly into another young person's voice message service and leave a voice message of their own. Voice messaging incurred no cost to the young person and was more personal than sending a text message.

*A.G.*: What is too much attention?

*Ayesha*: I dunno, when they try to touch[21] you or something.

*Melinda*: I don't like it when they try and fight [play fight] with ya, 'cos they're so rough, well the boys [Arms House Crew] who used to come here [youth club] anyway, they're too rough.

*A.G.*: But normally, you don't mind play fighting with boys?

*Ayesha*: Just messing about yeah, but they go too far. They fight, like they're fighting one of they're friends, they don't fight like they're fighting girls.

Manor Resource facility was not really suitable as a venue to run youth drop-in nights, compared to the nearby Woodhill youth centre[22], as the space available to the young people was very limited. The club was also under resourced in its equipment, staffing and general funding. Drop-in nights operated out of one room where there were two table-tennis tables and a small children's pool table—later on the centre was able to fund raise and buy a second hand pool table and dj mixing equipment[23]—as well as a Sony Play Station that belonged to one of the part time youth workers. In reality Manor centre was mostly suited for work with toddlers, children and formal education projects (as a result of the training room situated at the back of the centre) as opposed to young people, and this unsuitability was greatly illustrated by the activities of the Pups.

The Pups were regular attenders of the youth club and were renowned for their exuberance, high jinx and excessive amounts of energy. As the centre ran playgroups, and after school clubs—in two designated areas (under 5s space, 5-11s room) that were out of bounds to all young people—there were children's pictures on the walls, small toys and games scattered around the floors, and each group had their own cupboards stocked up with food in the kitchen. Yet every night the Pups would run about the building playing football, play-fighting (usually this involved them wrestling and jumping around on the children's inflatable mat), or just being a general nuisance. They particularly derived great pleasure from illicitly entering the children's play areas, where they would proceed to break lighting fixtures, tear down pictures, break toys and steal (along with the other young people) the children's food from the kitchen cupboards. I

21  'Touch' here is when young men grope young women in a sexually inappropriate manner.

22  There was a purpose built two storey statutory youth centre (built in 1986 and run by the local borough council) situated next to Manor in the adjoining neighbourhood of Woodhill. Woodhill youth centre featured a large in door sports hall, and a variety of rooms where the young people could get involved in a variety of arts, dance and music projects.

23  Comprising two turntables, mixer, amplifier, loudspeaker boxes and a microphone.

found myself continually nagging and moaning at the Pups to the point where they would say, that I 'moan too much', and that I should just 'chill out and relax' more, 'like before'[24].

A typical evening at the youth club involved the Arms House Crew going through the nightly ritual of refusing to pay the 25 pence entrance fee. The lines of argument were lifted from the same script and went along the lines of: 'give us a bligh[25] tonight, I ain't got no money, serious man' or 'I'm only holding a note (£20 note), I'll sort yous out later' (presumably after they have got some smaller change) or that one of their crew (who had paid the entrance fee) and who was already inside the club had money and would pay for them. This scenario might continue for up to an hour as they mulled about outside hoping that they would wear us down (youth workers) with their persistence so that we would just let them in without having to pay. Eventually, they would pay the fee (usually one of their mates who had money would pay for everybody to enter the youth club) and make their way straight toward the dj music room. Manley (black, aged eighteen and the self appointed 'rude boy' leader of the Arms posse) would usually head for the table tennis table or else dive onto the inflatable mat and proceed to single handily take on (or wrestle with) all of the Pups. The rest of the Arms House Crew would be busy causing mayhem in the music room (which at best could only hold eight young people) where at any one time there might be fifteen to twenty young people in there all grabbing the microphone and mc-ing[26] whilst Gato, Solo or B-line, cut and mixed up the latest underground garage/grime tunes. Sitting around chatting, laughing and flirting with the Arms crew would be the Poppettes, whilst the Pups (in between playing pool, table-tennis and wrestling on the mat) would verbally tease Manley and the other older Arms boys and end up being chased around the youth club by them.

## Public spaces IV: Raving

The term 'Raving'[27] as used within this study, is distinct from the phenomenon of Rave dance culture which involves 'dancing at mass all-night events, synthesised techno music with a heavy repetitive beat and the use of the class A controlled

24  'Like before' refers to the time before I became a centre-based youth worker, when I worked with the pups on the streets as a detached youth worker.
25  'Bligh', here refers to giving someone a 'break', or to 'let this one go, just this once'.
26  Mc-ing, where the young people rhythmically talk (or rap/toast) over records in order to get a crowd in a rave 'lively' and 'hyper'. Usually the mc will talk about how great he, his crew and his dj are, or tell the dj to play a hot record (rewind selecta) again and again as the crowd are loving it.
27  Raving is a black British term (derived from Jamaica) that has traditionally been used to refer to going out either to a 'dance' either at a shebeen, night club, or house party to listen to music, dance and basically forget about all your troubles.

drug, Ecstasy [MDMA]' (Muncie, 2004: 194). In contrast to those studies of contemporary Rave dance cultures (see Redhead, 1990; Redhead, 1993; Saunders, 1995, Thornton, 1995, Malbon, 1998; Reynolds, 1998), I am not too concerned with detailing the intense sensual and communal experiences of 'clubbing', or the pleasure of being with other people brought about largely through the combination of mood enhancing drugs, lighting effects, and music. Within this chapter, I present Raving (as with the youth club) as another important facet of 'road youth culture', albeit a more expensive one, where music (UK Garage) and dancing (as opposed to 'hanging about' and 'catching joke on road') takes centre stage.

As previously stated, road culture in Manor is mainly driven—both sonically and aesthetically—by the musical soundtrack of UK Garage along with MTV Base and Channel U video culture[28]. According to Simon Reynolds:

> Sometime in late 1996/early 1997, a segment of London's jungle audience began to wonder why they were listening to such dark, depressing music. Jungle had been shaped by the desperation of the recession-wracked mid-nineties; now, with 'loadsamoney' in their pockets, the junglists didn't feel desperate anymore ... Searching for a sound that better reflected their affluence and insouciance, the ex-junglists built a brand new scene based around the 'finer things in life'—designer label clothes, flash cars, champagne, cocaine, and garage music ... As well as attracting upwardly mobile, 'mature' white clubbers ... garage's mellow opulence had long appealed to junglists ... For most of the nineties, home-grown UK garage had slavishly imitated American producers. But when the ex-junglists entered the fray, they created a distinctly British hybrid strain that merged house's slinky panache with jungle's rude-bwoy exuberance.
>
> (Reynolds, 1998: 418-419)

To many of the informants, UK Garage is important because it is the soundtrack for their generation, what is more, it is a contemporary musical form that was created and nurtured in their hometown of London:

*Eddie:* I like most types of music, R'n'B, hip-hop, but I love my garage, that's the music we rave to. It's era music, our music. I mean people say

---

28  MTV BASE and Channel U are digital satellite video music channels to dedicated to US and UK 'urban' musical forms, style and fashion; notably Hip-Hop, contemporary R'n'B, Grime, Bass-Line, and Jamaican Bashment

this and that about how it will soon disappear, but no matter still, it's holding on strong.

*A.G.:* Why do people say that it will soon disappear?

*Eddie:* Mostly, I think 'cos they don't understand it. I mean don't get me wrong, from the time it hit the charts I knew that something was wrong, because garage is supposed to be the sounds of the underground. It's a music you make in your garage with your mates, hook up a few beats on the computer with a little mixing of sounds. But with technology and that, it sort of got better, and then it sort of went, I dunno, Pop [music].

*A.G.:* Why is it a bad thing for the music to get into the charts?

*Eddie:* Look at Artful Dodger [referring to a big underground record from a few years ago] that to me was so underground, I didn't see how that tune could end up in the charts, 'cos for me that's not where it belongs. I was disgusted sort of thing, and even when I listen to it now, it's like they've taken something away by them putting it in the charts, I dunno, I can't explain what they've done to it, but its, they've taken something away from it. It doesn't have its sparkle, 'cos to me that tune was about us, how we are when we're raving in a club, but I don't think half the people who know that tune now [through Pop charts] really know what its about. I mean kids that are four years old or six years old, they don't know what 'bo' means, but still they can sing along to the song. I mean for me when you say 'bo', what your saying is [that tune is the lick] or whatever, [that tune is just right]. Bo doesn't even have to be about that tune, it can be about anything. You can say bo when the dj does a wicked mix, and you understand that, but kids that are hearing the tune and singing the words and that, they can say the words but they don't understand the actual meaning, and for me that's not enough. Its like Motown, I listen to it, and I think I understand it, but I don't really because it isn't me, it wasn't my era. But when people tell me 'oh yeah, rewind' [Artful Dodger record], I think to myself 'no disrespect to you, but no this ain't for you, this ain't your era'. I mean, I'm not trying to push anyone out of my era, 'cos it's not just mine and anyone can be involved, but don't say you understand when you don't understand.

But for the overwhelming majority of young people, Garage music is the Raving music of choice:

*Mr. Business*: I like Garage, that's definitely me, yeah go out to a club check a few swirlies[29] and that.

*Maria:* On the weekends we [Poppettes] always go out to clubs, Zoom [night cub] everywhere really, we've been everywhere ain't we? [to Kandy]

*Kandy:* Venue, Harlequins, Country Club, Legends [Barking] when Deja' was there [pirate radio station].

*A.G.:* What music do you normally like Raving to?

*Maria:* I like Garage.

*Kandy:* Black music.

*Both:* Garage, R'n'B.

*Kandy:* I like Pop music I don't like Indie, I don't like Ibiza music erk I don't like.

*A.G.:* What about all that Pop music you used to like, like Boyzone ?

Maria: You know, I will always like Backstreet Boys [American Pop boy-band], I don't know why, but I just love their songs.

*A.G.:* You used to like Five [British Pop boy-band] as well.

*Kandy:* I like Five.

*Maria:* Yeah, nah I don't really like Five, I just like Jay out of Five.

*A.G.:* So how can you like Five on a Pop level and then like heavy Garage?

*Maria:* I dunno, it's just a certain type of music.

*Kandy:* I love Garage, I used to hate Garage so much but now I love it.

*Maria:* Garage is the music you dance to, like R'n'Bs the music you like lay down and listen to, and Pop music's when you're in bed and doing your hair.

Although the majority of young people are into UK Garage, like those informants quoted above, most will also enjoy listening to contemporary black American urban popular music. Therefore, most clubs or private/house parties will usually also have a smaller room dedicated to R'n'B and a limited amount of Hip-Hop and Bashment[30]. Even for those young people who might naturally prefer other types of music, the reach and pull of UK Garage (most of their friends will be Garage Heads) is in the main all too powerful:

29  Swirlies is a male road cultural term for young women and girls.
30  Bashment or 'Ragga'/'Dancehall' is a contemporary popular Jamaican music form.

*Little Man:* I don't mind Garage yeah, if it's in a Rave then I don't mind Garage, but I listen more to Hip-Hop in my house when I'm just relaxing, watching MTV Base, yeah that's definitely me.

*Griot:* I listen to all types of music, but specifically yeah, I say that I'm more into R'n'B. I don't mind a bit of Ragga, Soca or Garage. I'd rave to anything man, I don't have no limitations. I listen to all different kind of things, but really and truly it all depends on where you are and the people that you're with. Like if I was with the boys [Safe Crew] most of the time they like going to Garage Raves and that. Whereas I suppose, if I was in a mixed group [black male and female friends from college] we'd rather go to a Soul place, you know somewhere that plays R'n'B and a bit of Hip-Hop and Ragga or whatever. 'cos when your with girls now, you wanna try and cater for them as well, so we just more mix and match really.

As well as the music, most young people enjoy Raving because it affords them ample opportunity to meet different people and make new links.

*Melinda:* We're not old enough to get into the big raves yet.

*Ayesha:* Like Coliseum[31] and that, but we go to one's like one's in Hillside like the Venue.

*Melinda:* Legends … We go there and reach there about eleven ennit, sometimes we don't get in 'cos we're not eighteen, but most of the time we do. We go there, buy drinks, like see whose there, dance, just dance ennit.

*Ayesha:* Just mingle and meet new people.

*Melinda:* Meeting new boys and meeting new girls.

*Ayesha:* Yeah flirting with the boys.

*A.G.:* Would you look to become involved with the boys you meet there or are you only interested in them as friends?

*Ayesha:* I dunno it depends how they come across when you first meet them. If they come across like they're really sly and sneaky, then nah and you just dump their number [telephone]. But if they come across like genuine then it's alright, might ring 'em whatever, link 'em.

*A.G.:* What does link 'em mean, go out with them?

31 Coliseum—nightclub based in South London that used to run a legendary UK Garage night on a Sunday.

*Ayesha:* Go and meet them, like ring 'em up and say yeah [come meet me] we'll do whatever.

*A.G.:* What one-to-one or in a group?

*Ayesha:* Yeah one-to-one.

*Melinda:* No sometimes in a group.

*Ayesha:* Yeah, if they're with they're friends or whatever, then we go with our friends like, probably go round one of they're houses or if they got a car, go out in the car. Yeah it all depends how old they are.

**Chapter Seven**

# Road culture II: Badness and rude boys in the neighbourhood

East London is a unique and particular sub region of the United Kingdom (see chapter two) where black and other minority ethnic settlers have adopted specific aspects of East End working-class vernacular culture. As the respective autobiographies of Cass Pennant (2002), and Nigel Benn (1999) illustrate, young black men—particularly during the past thirty years or so—have gained the grudging respect of their white male peers in the 'hard' racist (Husbands, 1982 and 1983; Hesse and Dhanwant, 1992; Bowling, 1998; Newham Monitoring Project, 1991) hyper-masculine and hyper-aggressive world of East London, as a result of their physical prowess as footballers, boxers, street fighters, football hooligans and villains. In an area where physical strength (dockworkers), and macho pride are attributes revered almost above everything else, black males have been able to cut a path for themselves due in no short measure to their willingness and ability to have a good old 'tear up'[1] as and when required. Consequently, East London—traditionally synonymous with crime, organised violent crime, football hooliganism and other deviant maverick masculinities—is a unique 'place' in which to explore the attitudes, behaviours and life style choices of those young black males ('rude boys') who operate (by perpetuating 'badness') at the extreme margins of road culture in Manor.

As outlined earlier in chapter six, for the majority of young people (including young black males) living in Manor, road culture is not about rebellion or hedonism, rather it is centred upon meeting up with friends, 'hanging on road', attending the youth club, Raving, looking 'links' and 'catching joke'; in essence road life is about friendships, routine and the familiar. Although this chapter is specifically concerned with exploring, what criminologists might refer to as the delinquent or deviant lifestyles of a select grouping of black young males who 'live pon road', it has to be noted that these individuals are a minority (albeit a very influential and powerful minority) who should not be taken as representative of black youth in general. Of course, if these marginalised and disaffected young men ('rude boys') are such a small minority, why devote an entire chapter to them, glamorising their violent and criminal activities? Surely, this will only serve to

---

1   'Tear up' is an East London term for having a good old fistfight on the streets or bar room brawl.

perpetuate the stereotype of black youth as the perennial criminal 'other'? (Keith, 1993). I am also aware that by focusing on what some might refer to as black male 'deviance' and 'criminality', this book itself is in danger of falling into a similar trap—of pathologising and demonising black youth and their subcultures—as have those studies[2] that I have previously critiqued (see chapter one).

In response to such criticisms, this study maintains that road culture is not solely responsible for negatively influencing the actions and attitudes of a minority of black male youth. It is a fundamental assertion of this study that many of those 'rude boys' that perpetuate 'badness', do so not because they are black and listen to Rap, Bashment or UK Garage (Sewell, 1997), or even because they are rebelling against 'white supremacist capitalist patriarchy' (Majors, 1989; Lea and Young, 1984), rather my research—which is not informed by the narrower theoretical concerns of criminology—accepts that there are innumerable social, economic, emotional and psychological variables at play which might explain why certain young males (black, white and mixed parentage) are drawn into a life of 'badness'. Nevertheless, I feel that it is important to describe 'badness' as it exists within road cultural life, particularly because it impacts greatly on the lives of the majority of young people (in one way or another) who reside in Manor and the surrounding neighbourhoods. Individuals involved in 'badness' can either terrorise a neighbourhood and its inhabitants or provide protection and 'back up'; in most cases 'rude boys' take up the dual role of neighbourhood bully as well as protector. Consequently, where chapter six concerned itself with the meanings and realities of road culture within the lives of the majority of young people, this chapter explores the way in which black masculinities are played out within the multi-ethnic urban environment of Manor and it's surrounds.

This chapter is thematically separated into two distinct yet interrelated sections. The first half will look to explore young people's perceptions of how 'badness' impacts (or not) upon their usage of public space; particularly focusing upon the necessary road-competencies and contacts that are required in order for young people in Manor to safely negotiate the potential dangers of their own neighbourhood as well as those 'other' localities. Here, I will also look to address the young people's perceptions of safety and danger in their own neighbourhood and attitudes toward visiting other 'places'.

---

2    See, Liebow, 1967; Wilson, 1978; Pryce, 1979; Cashmore and Troyna, 1982; Majors, 1989; Majors and Billson, 1992; Sewell, 1997.

Section two addresses the role and importance of 'badness' within road life in Manor, by exploring its influence upon the young men's attitudes, values, and behaviour. First, I will discuss the way in which the majority of black (and those white, and mixed parentage young men involved in road culture) young males involved with road life, look to appropriate certain aspects of 'badness' for reasons to do with survival, 'money-making', and transient and sporadic 'delinquent drift' (Matza, 1964). I will then go on to focus on the small minority of mainly young black men whose lifestyles centre around the perpetuation of 'badness', where I am mainly concerned with detailing their values, attitudes and the types of activities that these 'rude boys' might be involved in. Whilst this is not a criminological study, I will nonetheless be looking to relate much of the data concerning 'badness' and 'rude boys' to those relevant discourses and research around race/ethnicity, youth and crime. Finally, this section will explore the influence of 'badness' upon the young men's school to work transitions, specifically in relation to how it effects (or does not effect) their attitudes toward education, training and employment.

## Section one: 'Place(s)' of safety and danger

### Safety in our neighbourhood: Family, kinship and friendship networks

Many of the informants (as well as their parents) were born in the area—or very near to it—and had built up extensive local kinship, family and friendship networks. This was important for engendering a strong local identification, and helped with regard to feelings of 'safety' within own neighbourhood; this was also found to be the case in a number of empirical studies[3]. Whilst it was acknowledged that Manor was a 'rough' area, for some of those young people who lived there it was a 'safe area' perhaps because they were related to, or friendly with, those individuals who contributed to the area's notoriety:

> *Darlene:* My home area that's where I feel more safe, 'cos I know this area and I know the people.
> *Kanya:* I feel safe in Manor for the same reasons 'cos I know everyone, know the black people.
> *A.G.:* Where would you say do you feel most safe, which area?

3   See, Evans et al., 1996; Watt, 1998; Watt and Stenson, 1998; Reay and Lucey, 2000; Mumford, K. and Power, A. (2003)

*Ayesha:* Manor, I suppose 'cos you can go anywhere else and it's like no this area's bad, this area's bad, so I say Manor's the easiest place to live in but.

*Melinda:* Yeah, but everybody thinks Manor's bad who don't live here, everyone's like 'no we ain't going Manor'.

*A.G.:* Do you think it's bad in Manor?

*Ayesha:* It is bad.

*Melinda:* It is bad, but not for us 'cos we know everyone.

Ayesha: Not as bad as it could be.

*Melinda:* No one troubles us 'cos we live here ennit.

*A.G.:* So if you didn't live here what kinds of things might happen to you in Manor that are bad?

*Ayesha:* Mugging, get robbed yeah.

*Melinda:* Probably get jacked[4] yeah.

*Sweet Boy:* Living round here I don't get no trouble, in the area a lot of people know me, a lot of people know me, just like from around, I live in like Manor, around like Manor a lot of people know my cousins [notorious local rude boys] and that, so ...

*A.G.:* You don't get no agg [trouble]?

*Sweet Boy:* No.

*Eddie:* ... any area can be safe you know, but it's where you put yourself that matters. I mean if you put yourself in a room full of thieves, but you actually know the thieves and you grew up with them then you're not in any danger are you? But if your a person whose just come in the area and you don't know the thieves, you don't know the muggers, you don't know the whatever else, then to you its dangerous, but I mean I'm not saying I know dangerous people, because to me they're not dangerous they're just people that have done things, anyone can be dangerous ... to say I feel safe or unsafe is wrong, 'cos it's the people I've grew up with, well I've grew up with bad people and I've grew up with good people.

Yet not all of the young people in Manor felt 'safe' within their own neighbourhood. Those who did not have local family or peer support networks to call upon—and/or were perceived as 'weak' as opposed to being tough and street-smart—were vulnerable on the streets to bullying, robbery and violence by their

---

4   'Jacked' where a person is robbed for their personal possessions and threatened with physical violence, or where actual violence has taken place via the street robbery.

more dominant peers. Such informants were likely to have a more ambivalent attachment to local 'place'. Martin, admitted to not feeling safe within his own neighbourhood, particularly around the basketball courts and open play space, which is situated near to Grafters—one of the area's local housing estates:

A.G.: What about safety, do you feel safe like growing up in this area?
*Martin:* Yeah, I feel safe to come over the park like but if I go anywhere that I don't know, then I feel a bit nervous.
A.G.: Which areas might you feel a bit nervous?
*Martin:* Erm around Grafters [Estate] but now it's alright but I dunno.
A.G.: Why don't you feel safe around Grafters?
*Martin:* Because I heard about the shooting, and everyday when I went down there like to play basketball, I always got into a new fight.
A.G.: Do you think there are more bullies around Grafters?
*Martin:* Nah, but if I had something like better than them they'd probably try and take it off me or something like that, like one day we was playing basketball and I kept scoring past them and they pushed me against the wall like, this was years ago, but now I'm alright.

A few years ago Martin's older brother was also mugged on the Grafters Estate. So even though the Grafters Estate is part of Manor—Martin's own local neighbourhood—it may as well be in another locality, as he is subject to bullying and intimidation by his more dominant peers. Young people like Martin are less likely to develop wholly positive attachments to Manor, because sometimes they are more likely to view their own home territory as a 'place' of danger rather than 'safety'. Nevertheless, the environmental competencies developed by many young people enables them to both successfully negotiate their local neighbourhoods as well as to stay and feel safe—what Cahill (2000) refers to as 'street literacy'.

## Race and other 'places'

Whilst many of the informants held emotional attachments to local 'place' characterised by a strong sense of pride towards their neighbourhood, none of the Manor youth—black or white—could be said to live totally 'localist' existences. Here, a 'localist' existence refers to the notion that young people very rarely venture out of their immediate locality, perhaps as a result of transport

5   See, Westwood, 1990; Taylor et al., 1996; Webster, 1996; Watt and Stenson, 1998.

problems or concern with those dangerous 'other places' that exist beyond the relative safety of the local neighbourhood. Various studies[5] have shown of black and Asian youth that 'localism' has partly arisen as a result of the fear of racialised violence that might take place outside the 'safe' confines of the locality. All of the young black people in my study identified particular 'less-safe' East London neighbourhoods where they were more likely to experience racism:

A.G.: What about other areas where maybe you wouldn't feel socomfortable?

*Tall Boy*: I don't feel safe in Castle Hill because of the racism, there's this pub yeah, a couple of Saturdays ago I went to my friends house in Hill View and I caught the bus the wrong way and went to Castle Hill and that was the last stop, then the bus driver wouldn't take me back 'cos he was going to Reema Fields anyway, so I asked him to take me back and he said no, so I had to walk from Castle Hill, but I didn't wanna call my mom 'cos if she found out I was there, I would have got into 'nuff trouble, I must have walked past the pub now and the pub was still open, 'cos I thought that pubs shut at eleven [p.m.] or something like that, the pub was still open going on one [am], I got chased by NF [National Front], people dashing bottles and everything ... I ran back to my friends house yeah and I bumped[6] a cab home, every time I go there something happens to me, I don't go there anymore.

*Griot*: Like Bridge House and that yeah, they got to sort out their race problems down there 'cos there's supposed to be some really bad racist situations down there.

A.G.: Where, Bridge House?

*Griot*: Yeah and Whiteview and that yeah, I been through them places, I haven't seen of it but I've heard, and it's supposed to be quite bad, it's one of those things, but if it was my area I'd make sure something got done about it, 'cos I wouldn't live in an area where I had to live in fear, trust can't be like that.

A.G.: Where in this area would you feel safe and where might you feel less safe?

---

6   Bumped—refers to practice of hiring a cab and then on arrival at destination running off without paying fare.

*Will:* Well here what, it definitely ain't no Whiteview, definitely, I've already had too many experiences there, even when I was working with Trevor doing that stupid club thing to go to South Africa. Yeah and Hampton, had a few run ins [problems] 'cos obviously Lisa's [Will's girlfriend] got family down there, she's got two sisters down there, but boy I don't want my son taken there let alone me go there, where else, Bridge House.

*A.G.:* What 'cos of racists down there?

*Will:* Yeah, well come on you've seen the [both laughing] big Union Jack outside the house, and Carol's [Lisa's close friend] bang in the middle of it, the only black person there, nah some Africans have moved there now but still, Bridge House, wouldn't go there. Been there a couple of times with Michael [friend] though.

Yet whilst some of the black informants might have felt less safe in these other 'racist' areas, in general it did not prohibit them from visiting these places. Consequently, the localism that Westwood (1990) and Taylor et al. (1996) attribute to black youth in their respective studies, cannot be said to hold true for any of the respondents in this study. In Manor, the Arms House Crew are the only group that might tenuously fit into what Westwood (1990) refers to as a black 'nationalism of the neighbourhood'. Where it is argued that in many black areas, inner-city space becomes 'our streets' to be violently defended against outsiders such as the police or other white young men. Yet this definition of the 'nationalism of the area' is quite problematic with reference to Manor, as it is an area that is not particularly racially/ethnically or economically polarised, and is therefore quite distinct from those East London neighbourhoods where relatively recent research studies[7] have been undertaken. Indeed, many of the white young people within this study were also very much aware of those less safe other racist 'places':

*A.G.:* Which area do you feel most safe and like the least safe?

*Maria:* I dunno, I feel more at home in like Manor and Parkview [neighbourhood that border's Manor] but erm ...

*Kandy:* Whiteview[8] I don't feel safe in ... I don't know why, I just don't ... girls just think they're rough down there.

7    See, Hesse and Dhanwant, 1992; Cohen, 1996; Bowling, 1998; Back et al., 1999; Foster, 1999.

8    Whiteview is a neighbourhood that is very close to Manor and is historically renowned for high incidences of street level violent racism.

*Maria:* No girls get on my nerves down Whiteview, 'cos its all the white girls and you just have to have fights with 'em 'cos they try it all the time.

*A.G.:* Why do they try it though, how do they know you're from Manor or Parkview or whatever?

*Maria:* They just know.

*Kandy:* They just do.

*Maria:* They don't see us about, like when you look at someone like you can tell what area they're from.

*Kandy:* They're just racist people.

*Maria:* Yeah, very racist, that's just my experience.

*Kandy:* Slaggy, slaggy, Whiteview slaggy ... Whiteview slags, dirty fucking slags.

Within the setting of a major conurbation like London, the notion of 'localism' cannot mean the same as it would when describing life in a smaller Northern or South Eastern English Town. London can be said to be made up of a number of distinct neighbouring cities, towns and villages, where East London might 'subjectively' be defined as the 'one-class city' (Hobbs, 1988). The majority of young people in this study, although their movements and leisure activities might not have been limited to the local neighbourhood, were nonetheless restricted to specific 'other' localities within the 'one class city' of East London and the surrounds of Essex. Furthermore, many of these other 'localities' tended to be borough centred. Manor, is a neighbourhood that sits on the border of two East London boroughs and is also in close proximity to the boundary demarcations of a further two. As a result of Manor's unique geography, many of the young people within the neighbourhood can potentially attend schools that fall under any of the four local authorities. In the main most of the young people attend one of the four local secondary schools—of which three are in one borough—whilst a sizeable minority have chosen or have been forced (through being permanently excluded) to attend secondary schools more further afield. Those young people who live in Manor—like Raymond—but who also attended school away from the neighbourhood, tended to have friends and other social networks in those same localities also.

Raymond originally attended a secondary school that was local to Manor but after being permanently excluded from there, was forced to attend a secondary school much further away in Park Hill, a predominantly white neighbourhood close to Bridge House. Raymond was constantly having physical fights with them 'white racist boys' who lived in places like Park Hill and Bridge House, yet he never sought to avoid any of these 'dangerous' places. He had a very close black male friend who lived in Park Hill, consequently he tended to spend quite a lot of time at his mate's house, or going to house parties, raves and youth clubs in the nearby vicinity. Although Raymond is from Manor, he had an extended peer and social network in those other more traditionally 'racially dangerous' spaces, importantly this provided him with 'back up'[9], if any trouble kicked off with those 'white racist boys'. Many of Raymond's black and white peers in Manor would not feel as comfortable spending their leisure time in such notoriously hostile areas as Park view. This was borne out of the fact that, unlike Raymond, they did not have extensive social and peer networks to call upon in such localities if they found themselves in danger. Thus as found by Robinson (2000) in her study of street-frequenting youth, the divisions many of the young people within Manor made with regard to those places:

> in which they felt comfortable and those they found threatening/negative, formed the basis of, and were maintained through, the development of sociospatial networks (Robinson, 2000: 435).

## Other black 'places'

Many of the black respondents seemed more concerned about visiting other black 'places', which can be said to be borne out of their acceptance of essentialist and stereotyped news-media images that portray black youth (particularly young black males) as potentially dangerous and prone to criminality. Consequently, whilst Raymond may have been at ease travelling through much of East London even those less safe 'white' areas, he was much more wary of visiting those less safe notorious 'black' areas in either East, North or South London:

> *Raymond*: Well I definitely don't feel safe in Reema[10] 'cos there mans always looking to prove something, when you go Reema you have to go with 'back up', with a crew, if I have to go by myself then I got to be

9   'Back up' where you have your crew or friends (in numbers) to watch your back and fight with you in case of trouble with another crew.
10  Reema is a pseudonym for a neighbourhood in East London that is perceived to be a black ghetto by many of the young people who live in Manor.

carrying something [a knife, or other weapon] 'cos them man from Reema
will look to jack you.

   This is true for many of the black young males in this particular study who,
by and large, try to avoid situations where they will be around their black male
peers from 'other' areas, particularly from those more notorious parts of South
and North West London that are perceived as 'ghetto' or black areas. Within
the minds of many black young people living in Manor—and within certain
sections of the wider population—there are areas within London that are
seen as predominantly black, like Harlesden or Brixton, and with this comes
the perception that these 'places' are also violent and lawless, the same features
that blight and mark out the black ghettos of the U.S.A. and Jamaica. On
one occasion Raymond was telling me how he doesn't really like 'them black
boys from other areas, "cos they're always trying it'. Che' (Raymond's younger
brother) recently had his trainers 'robbed' whilst walking through Stonehill[11],
I subsequently asked him whether or not he intended to exact some kind of
revenge for what had happened? As usually there would be reprisals if something
like that happened locally in East London. Raymond said he knew who did it
but left it at that. He explained that the perpetuator was 'some boy from Ghetto,
I know he was from down South somewhere 'cos my cousin is from down South'.
This was the only situation where a younger family member could be robbed
locally but no reprisal had taken place, normally street logic—or what Anderson
(1999) identifies in his ethnographic study as the 'code of the street'—would
dictate that Raymond do something (using his back up) or he would lose face
in front of his peers and everyone would be 'trying it'[12] with Raymond and his
family, as they would be perceived as 'pussies'[13].
   Sweet Boy was categoric in his assertion that he would never travel up
'North, no way', as he doesn't like 'people (black people) from North, areas
like Tottenham, Harlesden and them sides'. North West London [Harlesden,
Willesden, Stonebridge Estate] had got a bad reputation amongst many of the
black youth in Manor, as it was perceived to be 'Yardie' gangland territory. Darlene,

---

11  Stonehill is a neighbourhood situated nearby to Manor, but sits on the border of North and East London.
    Young people in Manor though class Stonehill as North London.
12  'Trying it', where other young people will look to intimidate (verbally and physically) another young
    person, knowing that they have no 'back up'.
13  'Pussies' is here used as a term of derision used to denote weakness/effeminacy in another young male.
14  'Hoggish' a term used to describe people who are rude, ignorant and aggressive.

is also wary about travelling to these 'other' black areas, especially 'Brixton, 'cos some of the people there are 'hoggish'[14] so you just get scared like'. Yet not all of the black young people in this study were wary about travelling to other black neighbourhoods around London:

> *Kanya:* I think East London's the worst out of all the areas ... I prefer North London because ... I don't know there's more things to do down there ... more black heads, more black people, I think round here's alright but you can't get nothing, you know like music and hair stuff, things like that. When it comes to black music you have to go everywhere, got to go to Reema, Tottenham, North London, there's nothing at the top of your road.

Griot, unlike most of his black peers is comfortable travelling all around London—including the West End, Camden, Uxbridge and Wembley—and does not feel the need to have back up, he is much happier travelling through areas on his own:

> *Griot:* 'cos when you walk in a gang people just tend to categorise you like, you see a group of black boys, what you gonna expect? They're thugs they're up to something, there doing something wrong, so we don't usually walk in group plus the police just hassle you as well, so there's no point.

## Section two: Badness, rude boys and transitions

### Road culture, badness, and 'drift'

As previously discussed (see chapter six) within road culture the majority of young people occupy the centre ground, with a small minority ('rude boys') of young men taking up the extreme margins. Nonetheless, there is a great deal of fluidity and movement to and from the centre ground and the margins, by a sizeable number of young men. At some point or another, those young men who normally occupy the centre ground of road culture may intermittently become embroiled within the world of 'badness', perhaps through their associations (friendly and antagonistic) with 'rude boys', or as a result of drift' (Matza, 1964), where it is argued that young people's involvement in deviant and criminal activity is both transient and sporadic. Adapting Matza's notion of 'drift', I would argue

that the majority of black young men involved in road culture within Manor
are neither committed to the values of the non conformist 'rude boys', nor to
those of mainstream society. Consequently, many of those young black men who
normally hold up the centre ground, will also sometimes choose to dip in and out
of 'badness'[15] as and when they see fit, or more to the point, when a particularly
good opportunity arises for them to make some 'easy money'. Non-'rude boys'
involvement in money making scams—such as receiving commission for the
successful 'street sale' of a 'hot' mobile phone from the 'rude boy' who actually
stole it—also fits into the East End tradition of 'ducking and diving' (see Hobbs,
1988) and highlights the way in which certain marginalised groups of young
people can become involved within the informal labour market on the edges of
crime (see Foster, 1990; MacDonald, 1994; Craine, 1997).

The non-'rude boys' involvement in 'badness' might also arise as a result
of 'beef'[16] with another young man or crew, at such times it is imperative that
all parties involved are willing to 'back it', and bring the dispute to a violent
conclusion[17]:

> *Richie*: Street culture is now aggressive. They label it with black culture
> now, but that's another story, but it is aggressive, it's totally different and
> that's why I can't relate to them [black young men]—even though I work
> with young males now—sometimes I find it difficult to relate to certain
> things that they do. Their sense of reasoning is different. Like when we
> was gonna get into something like a fight, like if we had disagreements
> and that, and me and one of my crew had an argument, it was just [piss
> off] and what have you, but he walks his way and I walk mine. Today
> though, they wanna fight and kill each other. When you're talking to
> them, there's no sense of reason it's just gone totally haywire. It's like 'he
> did this and I'm not having it, and we're gonna rush him' and I just don't
> understand where it's coming from.
>
> (Richie, black male youth worker)

15  The 'badness' that the majority of young men will get involved in will be around buying (purchasing—or
    acting as middlemen—stolen goods from 'rude boy' acquaintances, friends and family members) and
    selling stolen goods like designer clothing, Sony Play Stations, car radios and DVD Players etc.
16  'Beef' is where a young person has a dispute or argument with another young person or crew.
17  Usually the violent conclusion will involve knives or other weapons and will probably end up with a crew
    or group of young men (backing their mate) rushing an individual or smaller group of young men.
18  Quash, (or squash), whereby young men will look to settle the dispute by threatening violence and maybe
    look to bring the situation to a violent conclusion.

As already noted above with regards to the situation concerning Raymond and his younger brother, if a young male seemingly fails to adequately 'back' or 'quash'[18] any of his disputes as and when they arise, he will subsequently be labelled a 'pussy' and from there on in will lose his 'rep' and be subject to constant bullying and harassment.

One evening in the youth club Sweet Boy was complaining about how 'some people ain't what I thought they was', he was referring to Raymond (who is a member of the Safe Crew who dips in and out of 'badness' as a result of his close friendships with 'would be" rude boys') whom he describes as 'easily led', as a result of his (Raymond's) hanging around with the 'wrong boys'. Sweet Boy informed me that Raymond's 'rude boy' friends were having 'beef' with another crew, and on one particular occasion T-Boy (Raymond's friend) was on his mobile phone to a rival crew saying how he was ready to 'back it' and that he had such and such young person with him; unfortunately although not present at that moment in time, Raymond's name was mentioned. A few days later the rival crew started going around the neighbourhood and 'fixing people up properly' ('rushing' and 'jacking' Raymond's friends), word got back to Raymond that he was in the frame, and he started to become extremely frightened. At this point street logic would determine that Raymond make the right noises, saying that he's 'ready' and that he will 'back' any impending 'beef'. Apparently, whilst Sweet Boy, Raymond and another young man were walking 'road', Raymond saw a member of the rival crew (Stylo), and instead of looking to 'draw arms' (pull out a weapon ready to fight), Raymond 'ignomiously' began to 'beg for mercy':

> *Sweet Boy*: Raymond was begging like, going to Stylo [please, please, sort it out], he was going on like a pussy ... I tell you Ant [to me] people ain't what they seem.

To Sweet Boy and his friend, Raymond had lost face as they had seen a weakness in him, particularly as up that point he gave the impression that he would 'back it' and that he was 'up for things' (defending his and his crews reputations). But this little episode showed Raymond to be nothing more than a 'pussy', in Sweet Boys eyes at least.

## Rude boys perpetuating badness

Many of the young people (featured in this study) as well as wider society have internalised the media representations of 'dangerous' black youth (see

Murji, 1999). Whilst some black young people are offended at such negative stereotypes and portrayals, there are a small number of informants who for their own personal reasons readily buy into those images of the 'sexy' but 'dangerous' young black 'urban rebel'. Whereas those of a more 'respectable' disposition—who Anderson (1999) refers to as decent youth—might look to disassociate themselves from the negative representations of deviant and lawless black youth:

> *Mikey:* Unfortunately its certain crews and that, that give all of us a bad name, I'm being honest yeah, but them man's need to fix up like.
> *AG:* Who, Arms House?
> *Mikey:* I ain't naming no names or nuttin' but, you know what I hate though Ants, it's people putting us all in the same bracket like, I hate that, trust we ain't all the same, all shady and up to no good. It bugs me when they [white people] see us on the [street] corner and they start getting all didgy and holding their bags, or they go on like we're all shotting [dealing drugs]. Just pure negativity when it comes to black youths, but like I said when you really check it me and them lot [Arms House Crew] we ain't the same. I'm going college, taking my driving lessons, they're on road the only thing they know is badness, that shit ain't for me.

At the same time there are many young males (many of whom might from time-to-time flirt with certain money-making aspects of badness) who are less condemning and judgemental of badness:

> *Rufus:* Me personally, I ain't really feeling being on Road and doing Badness. I mean yeah, I might do my little things and that, nothing to bad like, you know linkin' man's with certain things or shottin' a little weed whatever
> *AG:* What about the harder stuff?
> *Rufus:* Nah, nah I ain't into that shit, if some one wants some punk [skunk] I'll hook them up but that's it
> *AG:* Do you think it's out of order to shot coke and brown [heroine]
> *Rufus:* Broth' I ain't judging no one, I don't know their circumstances and that. But if you feel that's what you gotta do to do survive, then that's you ennit. Everyone's got to make their own decisions in life.

Of course there are a minority of rude boys who gain kudos and pride from their (or their friends) various illegal and violent activities being featured in the crime pages of the local newspapers and thus adding further to their 'rep' as a 'sexy' outlaw or up-and-coming gangster.

The majority of badness that takes place within Manor and it's surrounds is carried out by a small number of young males (or crews) who live the rude boy lifestyle. This lifestyle is characterised by the rude boys involvement in anti social and offending behaviour: Property Offences, theft from a house or shop and the taking and driving/riding away of a car or moped without the owners consent; Fraud, selling or using a stolen cheque book, credit or other bank card to obtain money from a bank or to purchase items; Violent Offences, snatched from a person a purse, mobile phone, bag, jewellery or other possessions, to hurt someone with a knife stick or weapon, or beat up someone to such an extent that medical help was required. (The above are categories of Offences as included in the 1988/9 Youth Lifestyles Survey, see Flood-Page et al., 2000). In addition to the above offences rude boys might also become involved in low-level drug dealing, operating on the bottom rung of drug supply ladder selling small amounts of crack cocaine, marijuana and heroin.

The most identifiable and notorious who live the bad boy lifestyle include: first, the Arms House Crew who have built up their 'reps' over a number of years—and; second, a fifteen year old prolific 'rude boy' named Simon Peters who, although loosely affiliated to the Pups, operated his own little crew of young 'bad boys' who were being taken under his protection.

### Arms House Crew

The Arms House Crew are a loose collective of African Caribbean young men (ages ranged from 17-21) who live around the Arms House area of Manor. They are made up of a core of about eight young men, but including up to another eleven individuals who are loosely attached to the crew. The Arms House Crew projected a tough, confident and streetwise group identity, and revelled in the fact that they were from Arms House. Arms House was a notoriously 'rough' part of Manor (at least in the eyes of those individuals who lived in the neighbourhood) and comprised a number of high-rise tower blocks and built up housing estates.

The key individuals of the crew were:

*Manley* (the self-appointed leader), an eighteen year-old;

*Nathaniel*, eighteen-years old black male;

*Redz*, a sixteen years-old black male;

*Makki*, an eighteen years old black male; and,

*Simon Peters* a fifteen years old male of mixed Caribbean and white
parentage who was loosely attached to pups. But the pups and someone
even Simon's older peers were wary of him.

*Raymond:* Simon, yeah, he don't care, he's a mad one. See, if he's got beef
with you, he's the type of bre'er that even if you beat him down, he will
come back later and start shooting a gun after you in your house, he's
just sick. He's a sick bre'er.

On the grapevine it was also said that he had cousins who were known
notorious 'rude boys' (from a nearby neighbourhood) and that they had paved
the way for him to 'carry on stink'[19] with impunity. Allegedly he had been with
them on a number of 'moves'[20] including the armed robbery of an off-licence.

### Jacking: Street bullying and robbery

Within this paper the term street robbery refers to the robbery or attempted
robbery of personal property and snatch thefts on streets or in public settings,
where victims are subjected to actual physical violence or threatened with
physical violence. There is a great deal of confusion with regards to defining
or ascertaining the true extent of street robbery offences. Interestingly, there
are a good number of individuals who view street crime, mugging and street
robbery as one and the same thing. Even more surprisingly, not one of the
above 'common-sense' descriptions actually describes an official criminal offence
category (Stockdale and Gresham, 1998). It is also rather difficult to assess
or measure the scale of the problem, as the majority of police forces within
England, Scotland and Wales do not compile statistics in relation to street
robbery offences.

Official statistics for robbery offences in England and Wales rose sharply
particularly during the late 1990s and early part of this decade (see, Fitzgerald, et
al., 2003, Smith, 2003), these increases were primarily attributed to the growing
problem of 'street crime' which is used by some police forces to describe personal
robbery and snatch thefts. Nationally across England and Wales, street crime
accounts for less than two per cent of recorded crime offences and three per cent

19  To take liberties and do as he pleased.

20  Moves—where 'rude boys' will go and perpetuate badness, usually a robbery of a shop or robbing a 'rude
boy' drug dealer (of his money and drugs) who they feel needs to be brought down a peg or two.

of BCS (British Crime Survey) crime during 2006/07, however, it is one of those categories of crime that the general public feels most apprehensive about.

Various research studies drawing upon official statistics and victim surveys have highlighted the over representation of young black males as street robbery suspects (see Harrington and Mayhew, 2001; and Fitzgerald et al., 2003; and Smith, 2003). However, as with the extrapolation of all crime statistics, data pertaining to the ethnic profile of street robbery suspects needs to be treated with extreme caution as the 'available street population within an area might not reflect the profile of its resident population ... a finding also confirmed in recent stop and search patterns' (Hallsworth, 2005: 58; see also Waddington, et al., 2004).

Nevertheless, whilst acknowledging the shortcomings of research based upon official crime statistics, Harrington and Mayhew's study exploring mobile phone theft does highlight a number of issues that reverberate within my own research, notably in explaining why mobile phones are stolen, apart from the key fact they are small and valuable commodities with ready made re-sale markets, they also touch on:

> a notion ... that phones are stolen in the process of 'taxing'. Here, the phone theft per se is less important than groups of offenders exerting control, establishing territorial rights and showing 'who's who' by penalising street users [in particular young ones] through phone theft amongst things. (ibid: 2001: 58).

This issue of 'taxing' or 'jacking' (also briefly discussed by Fitzgerald et al. 2003; and Hallsworth, 2005) is of great significance within Manor as it is the means by which many of the rude boys police the physical space of the neighbourhood by exercising control and dominance, particularly over their more vulnerable male peers. Most jacking is opportunistic and might easily be described as 'street bullying' and does not fit with the common-sense image of the young black male bag snatcher (or mugger) whom, it is argued (see Burney, 1990) undertakes this type of offence in order to fund an increasingly expensive lifestyle centred around acquiring the latest designer 'street wear' fashions. Bill Sanders' (2005) study about black, white and 'mixed-race' young offenders in a South London inner-city borough similarly concludes that:

… those more involved primarily committed serious acquisitive offences, such as robbery and burglary, with the intention of exchanging the stolen goods for cash … The money these young people earned from such offences went towards status enhancing items and activities they enjoy, such as 'looking good', eating out, smoking cannabis, and raving …

(ibid: 2005: 75)

Many of the rude boys featured in my research do not solely practice badness as a means of obtaining the trappings of 'style'. For young males such as Smokey and the various members of the Arms House Crew, badness entails maintaining and enhancing rude boy reputations and levels of respect (through the bullying and intimidation of other young males) among their peers within the neighbourhood and its surrounds:

AG: … so what sort of things might you and the rest of the Arms get up to on road?

*Mackie:* [to rest of crew] Anthony's a joker man … you know everything that goes on round here, we know you got your little informers [all start laughing]

AG: Ok, so if someone's on Road doing badness, what might be involved?

*Kai:* Depends on who they are. Some people are on road but they're just playing [faking it]

*Mackie:* For real

*Kai:* It's about juggling and runnings, we do whatever ennit. Shotting …

AG: Drugs?

*Mackie:* Not just that, anything that can make us a little change

*Jamesy:* Everything we do has to be on point. Can't be slipping or else you'll have next crews trying a ting and that. Man's are hungry out on road. Ain't nuttin for them to try and take your spot.

AG: In terms of running the neighbourhood?

*Mackie:* 'Course. We run Manor, we can't have no little pussy holes thinking they can take liberties. Man's supposed to be shook [scared] when they see us on the endz

*Kai:* Yeah, but shits bigger than Manor still, you've got next crews from all over, East London, North London, wherever, everyone's looking to get stripes off your back.

*Mackie:* True that, we juggle wherever we can make a little something. But it's all about the name [Arms House] as well.

*AG:* So then Badness is about runnings and maintaining your rep' then?

*Jamesy:* It's all about largin' up the rep, we ain't the Arms House for nothing. C'mon Ant even you must know that [all laughing].

## Theorising badness

The focus of this chapter has largely been concerned with exploring the role and impact of 'badness' upon the lives of young people living in Manor and it's surrounding neighbourhoods. This study is largely concerned with exploring black young men's school-to-work transitions, taking into account the influences of their peer group and family/home lives. As such my theoretical understanding of 'badness' differs greatly from those writers and researchers whose work is mainly informed by the narrower concerns and pre-occupations of criminology. I maintain that 'badness' is a lifestyle choice—involving the complex interplay of power, and control (via physical force), language, music, dress wear, and a youthful disregard of the values and institutions of mainstream adult society—that is adopted by a small minority of male youth, and is appropriated[21], in a cut'n'mix style, by even larger numbers of young people. Importantly, for me 'badness' is not just about delinquency or the effects and consequences of criminal activity, it is more about placing such adaptations and modes of being within the broader context of the young people's everyday lived experiences.

Contemporary criminological explanations of the causes of crime (or aspects of badness)—whilst not ignoring the many complex and subtly differentiated discourses around crime (and race) present within criminology—have tended to focus on the pathology and cycles of deprivation/amorality inherent within those cultures of the underclass (see, Auletta, 1982; Murray, 1984, 1990;). Alternatively they are reliant upon structural determinist interpretations of crime (as well as racism) via the concept of relative deprivation (see, Lea and

---

21  Of course there are sizeable minority of young people whose lives are negatively impacted upon as a result of the perpetuation of 'badness' in the neighbourhood.

Young, 1984; Taylor, 1981; Young, 1986) and draws upon liberal theories of delinquent youth sub cultural formation (Cohen, 1955). Both perspectives or 'realist' criminoligies:

> concentrate more on those crimes which are at the centre of public concern, namely youth crime, street crime, violence and burglary, than of crimes of the powerful or those crimes perpetuated by the state itself.
>
> (Muncie, 2004: 136)

According to left 'realists' such as Lea and Young (1984), black youth are pushed into the margins of society (and into a life of crime and relative deprivation) as a result of their access to the labour market being denied via racism and capitalism. In response to their exclusion from the social, economic and political institutions of mainstream society, black youth have created criminal sub cultures as a means of 'getting back' at the white dominant culture.

Whilst virulently disagreeing with the notion of 'criminal' black sub cultures, critical cultural theorists of racism and crime (Gilroy, 1982 and 1987b; Gordon, 1983; Hall et al., 1978; Sivanandan, 1982) argue that black youth are unfairly labelled by the media as criminals and then actually turned into criminals by the police, law courts and immigration authorities, as a result of institutionalised racism. Interestingly, whilst left realists look to blame changes in the globalised capitalist and political economy for the creation of criminal black youth sub cultures, critical theorists argue that 'racism and criminalisation are not ends in themselves, but the result of a specific crisis in the capitalist economy in Britain' (Bowling and Phillips, 2002: 65). Other more notable additions to the (black) youth crime debate draw on those discourses around hegemonic 'masculinity' (Connell, 1987), whereby class and race position combine to place certain young males at the bottom of the social and economic ladder. As a response to such marginalisation, black and other working class young males respond to their powerlessness by constructing sub cultures based around crime and other deviant modes of behaviour (see, Collier, 1998; Messerschmidt, 1993; Stanko and Newburn, 1994). Again the inference here is that such 'maverick' masculinities based upon deviance and criminality, are in the main still largely determined by structural crises within the racist-capitalist global and political economy.

Of course there is a sizeable minority of young people whose lives are negatively impacted upon as a result of the perpetuation of badness in the neighbourhood. Importantly, for me badness is not just about delinquency or the effects and consequences of criminal activity, it is more about placing such adaptations and modes of being within the broader context of the young people's everyday lived experiences. Even though many of the young black males flirt with badness, they are not career criminals who have created lifestyles around deviance and hyper-masculinity as a result of racism or social and economic marginalisation. Rather, they are at a point in their lives when they are discovering who they are and what they are about as individuals in their own right, they are looking to push the boundaries of adult society and do what most normal teenagers do—rebel. As Katz notes 'in many youthful circles to be bad, to be a [badass] or otherwise overtly to embrace symbols of deviance is a good thing' (Katz, 1988: 80), especially when the symbols, styles and aesthetics of badness are celebrated within contemporary popular culture via a plethora of bashment and hip hop songs and videos.

Indeed, Jock Young (2003) has more recently moved beyond his earlier versions of left realism in trying to overcome the over-reliance on Mertonian explanations of relative deprivation that stress the mundaneity of crime. Drawing on Katz's (1988) classic text and more recent developments within the field of cultural criminology, Young asserts that crime, rather than being mundane, has its:

> excitement, its drama, its seductions and punishment, like it, its vindictiveness, its hostility, its thinly concealed satisfactions. In contrast the criminology espoused by rational choice theory ... is quite simply the criminology of neo-liberalism and its truth claims are as limited as those that depict society as held together simply by contractual relations of a market place.                    (Young, 2003: 392)

Young and other writers working within the area of cultural criminology (see for example, Ferrell, et al., 2004) maintain that the values and seductions of badness are celebrated within popular mainstream culture, consequently acting them out behaviourally may be particularly appealing to those individuals and subcultures operating at the margins of society. Wright, et al. (2006), in their study which looked at the situational dynamics of street robbery in the United Kingdom, also noted that whilst offending behaviour was largely motivated by a need to obtain money, it was 'activated, meditated and channelled by participation in an emerging street culture in Britain … linking criminal motivation to subjective situational conditions' (ibid, 2006: 2).

## Transitions into badness

Most of the young men involved with road culture tend to 'drift' (Matza, 1964) in and out of 'badness' with regard to their involvement in 'beef', and money making scams through handling 'jacked goods'[22] and selling them on to a third party at a profit. They may also adopt those more uncompromising 'rude boy' attitudes and values 'of not havin' it', whereby they are not prepared to be 'chiefed off' by being 'spoken to in a way' by no racist teachers, police officers, potential employers or any other figures of authority (including sometimes their parents). Many of the young black males (and indeed their female counterparts) in this study demand that they are treated fairly and spoken to with respect by adults; if on the other hand these same young people feel slighted or 'dissed' by adults in authority, then it is more than likely that conflict and confrontation will ensue. Black male youth in Manor are most likely to 'drift' or flirt with certain aspects of 'badness' as a result of conflict and problems in school, which in certain cases results in their being permanently excluded (see chapter four). Again, reasons for conflict within school might be as a result of on-going 'beef' with another young person which has spilled over from road life into the classroom, but more than likely it stems from the young men's dis-interest and alienation from both school and teachers. Road life is about action, movement (running, walking street or about playing sports) excitement, fun and to a certain extent freedom—in as much as the young people have the money or access to specific leisure opportunities—for the young people in this study road culture represents real life, as they must learn to rely upon their wits and street-smartness in order to avoid danger, make money, 'links' and 'catch joke'. School on the other hand is about rigidity, inaction, boredom, irrelevance and 'rude' teachers who on the whole seem not to be able to relate to the worlds in which much of Manor youth inhabit.

As a consequence of problems with school (exclusions or bad reports) and general flirtation with 'badness', it is more than likely that many of the young men will also then get into conflictual situations within the home, perhaps resulting in a break down in the relationship between themselves and their parents (see chapter five). A family crisis situation like this, which is all too common, will further serve to push the young person even deeper (usually

22 'Jacked goods' are items that have been stolen from individuals through robbery e.g. stolen mobile phones.

only temporarily) into road culture and particularly 'badness'. Even though many of the black young men flirt with 'badness', they are not career criminals who have created lifestyles around deviance and hyper-masculinity as a result of racism or social and economic marginalisation. Rather, they are at a point in their lives when they are discovering who they are, and what they are about as individuals in their own right, and are looking to push the boundaries of adult society, and do what most normal teenagers do—rebel. All of the black young men featured in this study expressed to me their strong desire to obtain for themselves a decent education, a good job and to eventually settle down and have a family. Unfortunately, many of them, for a variety of complex reasons (see chapter four) find it difficult to successfully make the transition from school to further education, work based training or indeed paid employment. Research has shown that those young people not involved in education, employment or training (NEET) at age 16-18 are less likely 'grow' out of crime (or stop flirting with aspects of 'badness'), and more importantly throughout the course of their life, in comparison to the rest of the population, they are more likely to face higher rates of: unemployment; poverty; alcohol and substance mis-use; ill-health; poor and overcrowded housing conditions; teenage pregnancy and limited intergenerational mobility.[23]

Whilst their mainly white peers who are more involved in Grafter culture, will normally drop out of education and find work as labourers or semi-skilled manual workers (a very small minority of them are fortunate enough to obtain apprenticeships, usually via familial contacts, as electricians, carpenters and plumbers), black young men will normally enrol on vocational courses at college (before dropping out altogether) or obtain (sporadic) part-time or casual employment within the clean non-manual service sectors (sports retail shops, telephone sales) or else endeavour to make a full-time career from perpetuating 'badness' on road. 'Rude boys' feel compelled to 'live on road' because it affords them excitement, and ample opportunity to make quick money and the chance to be 'somebody', to be respected and feared amongst their peer group. Whilst many of these black young men (small minority of rude boys) are from relatively deprived socio-economic backgrounds, I feel it would be wrong to solely use structural determinist (or relative deprivation) arguments as a means of explaining their involvement with crime and 'badness' (Lea and Young, 1984; Taylor, 1981). Likewise, those writers who rely upon liberal theories of deviant

23  See, Blundell et al., 1999; Social Exclusion Unit, 1999; Flood-Page et al., 2000; Ermisch and Francesconi, 2001; Coles et al., 2002.

black youth subcultural formation—as nihilistic and rebellious responses to white racist society—in order to theorise about the perennial 'problem of black youth'[24] fail to take into account a number of other interrelated psycho-social as well as economic variables.

Many of those young black males in this study who I refer to as 'rude boys' are perceived as being 'sick bre'ers' by their peers, where the common consensus of opinion is that such youth are 'mad' or 'not normal' because they are prepared to do 'off-key'[25] things that most 'normal' young people would never think about undertaking. Consequently, a 'mad one' will throw a desk at a teacher or is known for 'bore-in'[26] other young people. Whilst the majority of young people will not condone their 'mad' friends violent and erratic behaviour, neither will they condemn it either; the most likely reaction to 'sick' behaviour is that of mild amusement and entertainment, more information with which to 'catch joke'.

24 Cashmore, 1982; Pryce, 1979; Majors, 1989; Sewell, 1997.
25 Off-key, in the eyes of the young people refers to irregular or abnormal 'mad' behaviour, like excessive violence, rape or paedophilia.
26 'Bore-in', the young people are here referring to the carrying and using of knives or other sharp objects by individuals to stab and wound others.

## Chapter Eight

# A few last words

This brief chapter is not intended to be a final conclusion to this study, as like all research, it is still a work in progress; the lives of those young people who participated continues apace regardless. Furthermore, I have not attempted to provide neat and tidy answers to those questions that have been raised through this study. Rather this research project has been more concerned with offering insights, and not solutions, into the black youth question. There are those writers and practitioners—within the media, the academy, and various public bodies—who might feel that I should perhaps provide policy recommendations within this chapter, aimed at arresting black young men's increased social marginalisation. I will avoid all such suggestions by reminding the reader that this study has attempted to 'de-essentialise' its black male subjects, by highlighting the fact that they are all unique individuals with their own personal biographies, hopes, dreams and frustrations. Moreover, I will reiterate the fact that my black male informants' outlook on life and everyday experiences are informed by their local environment, family situation, peer group and road subcultures, as much as by their gender and ethnicity. Any researcher who does presume to formulate policy suggestions in relation to young black men, will need to be mindful of the above key (and interdependent) determinants which inform their day-to-day experiences.

Manor is a multi-ethnic neighbourhood where black, white and mixed parentage young people live (and grow up) on the same housing estates, attend the same schools, 'hang out' together, and share similar family backgrounds. From such shared experiences young people in Manor develop interracial friendships and road cultures centred upon music, dress, and leisure activities—which in turn largely informs their attitudes and behaviour. However, whilst there is a commonality of experience that exists between both black and white working-class young people in Manor, locality and class position does not account for their total life experiences. Black young people have a distinct cultural heritage which partly explains their differing (in comparison to their white working-class peers) experiences within the education system, and the higher incidences of police harassment and rates of unemployment amongst this particular ethnic grouping. Consequently, many black and white young people will embark upon completely different career paths on leaving school at sixteen. The vast majority of my informants left secondary school with little or no formal qualifications, and expressed some regret at this missed educational opportunity. One of the main findings of this study was that the majority of my white male informants (and small minority of black young males) left school and obtained full time paid employment within the building and construction industries. Therefore, contrary to the findings of many of the youth-as-transitions studies in other regions (Banks et al., 1992; MacDonald, 1997; Meadows, 2001; McDowell, 2004), within this study I maintain that some white working-class young men are still continuing to make traditional school-to-work transitions in spite of economic restructuring within the London East sub-region.

In contrast to widely held assumptions and stereotypes about black youth, the majority of my black male informants on leaving school at sixteen looked to engage with mainstream society by enrolling on vocational type college courses whilst undertaking part-time paid employment within the service and voluntary sectors. Rather than inhabiting deviant subcultural worlds—characterised by hyper-aggressive and hyper-masculine attitudes and behaviour (Pryce, 1979; Cashmore and Troyna, 1982; Sewell, 1997) and the 'cool pose' (Majors, 1989 and 1990)—the black young men in this study had high hopes and ambitions for their futures. Since leaving school the majority of my female informants (black, white and mixed parentage) also enrolled on full-time college courses whilst working as part-time shop assistants, receptionists, bar workers, or attendants at the local leisure centre.

Road culture stresses the need for those involved in it to 'look slick' (well dressed) and not be seen as 'weak' or as 'pussies', whereas working on a building site and undertaking manual labour is seen by many young people as 'dirty', 'back breaking' and 'dead end' work. Consequently, by going to college, my informants expressed a desire to obtain 'upwardly mobile' careers within 'clean' office environments in such hi-tech fields of engineering, computing, and information technology. Those white young men who moved completely away from road culture on leaving school to 'graft' for a living, were following in the masculinist working traditions of their fathers, uncles and grandfathers. Manual labour afforded them the opportunity to become 'men' and provided them with an income with which to purchase cars, settle down with their girlfriends, take holidays abroad, and undertake pub-centred leisure activities. Most importantly, honest full time 'graft' pulled such working-class young men away from those alternative career paths involving petty crime, 'joy riding', and street level violence (Parker, 1974).

The much smaller number of black young men who opted for alternative career paths, through their involvement in 'badness', were not pulled into a life of violence and petty crime as a result of the negative influence of road culture. Such individuals were viewed as 'sick bre'ers' (by their peers) who looked to push 'road life' to the limits. Whereas most young men exercised caution and 'road sense' with regards their involvement in 'badness', others became deeply attached to the dangers, excitement and kudos derived from living 'on road' as a 'rude boy'. There are many—complex and interrelated—social, emotional and psychological reasons why a small number of young men were prepared to be pulled into the extreme margins of road culture. However, this study maintains that it is misleading to view 'badness' and rude boy attitudes and behaviour solely in terms of the causal effects of institutionalised racism (relative deprivation), or the negative influence of road culture.

Most of the young women in this study avoided becoming directly involved in 'badness', preferring to 'hang about' and 'catch joke' with the 'rude boys' on road', or at raves. Significantly, unlike many of their older peers (such as the Young Moms and Sweatshop Girls.), all of my female informants had avoided the alternative career path of teenage motherhood. Whilst discussing the impact and significance of 'badness' with regards to life 'on road', this study maintains that road culture is more about the humdrum and the mundane rather than the 'spectacular'. Road life for my informants is about 'hanging about' and 'killing time', 'catching joke', 'looking links' and wearing 'nice garms'. Those more spectacular aspects of road culture are linked to the styles, attitudes and behaviour associated with 'badness' and 'rude boys'.

The majority of young black men—and their close white and mixed parentage friends—'drift' (Matza, 1964) in and around the periphery of 'badness' by getting involved in 'beef' with other young men, and various money-making 'scams'. Such young men will also tend to walk around 'on road' in small groups wearing designer sports wear, looking menacing and aggressive to both adult outsiders and potential foes (their peers). Unfortunately, to the outside world the black young men of Manor—who hang about in small groups wearing hooded sports tops and talking loudly whilst 'hogging' the pavement—are indistinguishable from the small minority of 'rude boys' or other black male youths growing up in the numerous urban and sub urban multi-ethnic neighbourhoods throughout England. However, this study maintains that whilst sharing a commonality of experience based upon gender and ethnicity, it is misleading to view black British young males (or females) as a single homogenous entity, as their experiences are differentiated by the political economy and cultural influences of local 'place', family background, personal psychology, and schooling. Nonetheless, there is a dearth of British based empirical youth research that holistically explores black young people's experiences growing up within their local neighbourhoods. This study has attempted to address this issue and I feel has helped to hopefully kick-start the process.

When I began this project I was bewildered as to why there was such a dearth of empirical and holistic British based research studies undertaken with young people. The problem I feel lies in the fact that youth studies within Britain has tended to be polarised between either youth subcultural studies, on the one hand, and youth-as-transitions on the other (Cohen and Ainley, 2000; MacDonald et al., 2001). Also, apart from being time consuming and very demanding, holistic empirical youth studies require the researcher to abstain from 'jumping into bed' with any one theoretical discourse. Unfortunately, academia is rife with petty and competing theoretical fiefdoms to which impressionable (and pragmatic) PhD candidates are required to subscribe. Those researchers who are interested in race and ethnicity will usually undertake theoretically driven research studies that explore hybridity, urban multi-culture and 'new' racisms. Also the few black research students that do manage to slip through the academic net, on the whole, tend to be concentrated within the areas of cultural studies and educational studies; and thus take on the more narrow theoretical and/or practice-based research concerns of these disciplines.

No doubt, I will be asked to tie my colours to one theoretical mast, on this I shall pass and maintain that in order to undertake holistic youth research this study has shamelessly borrowed—in a cut 'n' mix style (Hebdige, 1987)—from an array of different and competing theoretical perspectives. I am very much aware of the fact that this study only offers brief snapshots of my young informants' complex lives, as I had 'access to only part of who they are, might be, or might become' (Ball et al., 2000: 20). Ball et al. further maintained that their study was not the sort of study that generates a simplistic set of concrete conclusions, however, there was one crucial exception: 'differences in social class participation in post-16 routes and the confirmation of class reproduction for many' (ibid: 143).

Within this study I cannot and do not provide for any crucial exceptions to the fact that I have not provided a simple set of firm conclusions with which the reader might better understand my informants' lives. I do not feel that this study presents sufficient evidence to indicate whether or not social class—as opposed to race/ethnicity (racisms), 'place' or gender—was the most significant factor with regards my informants' lifestyle and post-16 choices and opportunities.

It would be all to easy to attempt to draw a number of tenuous conclusions from this study, however, such conclusions would be informed more by my own theoretical biases and pre-occupations than on any concrete empirical data. For instance, it is possible to argue that social class was the most significant influence with regards to the Grafters lifestyles and transitions. As outlined in chapter four, whilst East London has seen the demise of many of its key industries over the past thirty years, the majority of my white young male informants have benefitted from the construction boom generated by the development of the Docklands. On leaving school at sixteen, members of the Grafters managed to secure full-time paid positions as labourers, builder's mates, forklift truck operators and apprentice electricians on City and Docklands construction sites. Hence, such young men's continued participation within the world of paid manual labour could be said to be a confirmation of social class reproduction for the Grafters—thus illustrating how some working class youth still get working class jobs (see Willis, 1977).

On the other hand, it is possible to view race/ethnicity as the single most influential factor impacting upon my black informants' lifestyle and post-16 choices and opportunities. As a result of institutionalised and popular racism as experienced by black young people within school and at street level (including police harassment), it could be claimed that in response they have developed attitudes and modes of behaviour (informed by road culture), which are anti-(white) authority. It can be further argued that the black young people in this study, as with their peers throughout the country, refuse to put themselves through the ordeal of attempting to enter a racist youth labour market at sixteen years-old where they will face unequal treatment at job interviews in comparison with their white peers. Even those few black young people who are fortunate enough to find full time paid employment will then have to endure the indignity of being 'bossed about by some racist old white fool'. Consequently, individual black youth are consciously extending their transitions by attending college or else bypassing mainstream society by working full-time 'on road'. Bell Hooks (1992 and 2004) argues that African-American men have historically resisted the norms of neo-colonialist white supremacist capitalist patriarchy:

black males whose brute labor had helped build the foundations of
advanced capitalism in this society had never been paid a living wage.
Work had never been for them the site where patriarchal manhood could
be affirmed ... More than any other group of men in this nation black
males have realistically understood wage slavery. They have been far less
likely than other groups of men to believe that employment will lead to
self-esteem and self-respect.                    (Hooks, 2004: 19-21)

African-American males have traditionally sought to avoid the low pay and
the indignities and daily disrespect of work-place racism by creating meaningful
alternative work arenas. Professional sports and the world of music are two such
sites of possibility, locations where alternative forms of black masculinity could
be formed and expressed. Not all those black males seeking alternatives to the
white supremacist capitalist patriarchal norms of waged labour are talented
enough to succeed in the worlds of music or sports, and have therefore turned
toward the illegal street economy of drug dealing, hustling and violent crime.

By adopting Hooks' theoretical perspective it is possible to assert that black
British (particularly male) youth like their African-American cousins have
inherited alternative strategies with which to deal with the white supremacist
capitalist evils of waged labour. Furthermore, unlike their white working-class
peers black male youth cultures have never viewed the attainment of full-time
paid employment as being particularly desirable or self-affirming. Above I have
attempted to play devil's advocate by asserting the singular importance (impact)
of either social class or race/ethnicity upon my informant's lifestyle and post-16
career choices and opportunities. However, I do not feel that there is sufficient
evidence contained within this study to substantiate such claims. Moreover,
such assertions essentialise both black and white young people whereby they are
represented as homogeneous automatons rather than individuals with unique
personal biographies informed by gender, race/ethnicity, place, social class,
family-home life and personal psychology. It is important that the conclusions
arrived at do not overemphasise macro structural constraints with young people
represented largely as victims and not as individuals and social actors (Beck,
1992; Giddens, 1991) who are able to self-govern their own lives in spite of the
prevailing wider political and socio-economic conditions.

Significantly, this study attempts to explore the complex ways that young
people attempt to self-govern their own lives whilst taking into account the
macro structural influences of social class, race/ethnicity, and gender. I adopt

Matza's (1964) notion of 'drift' in order to explain how the majority of my black male informants will sometimes choose to dip in and out of 'badness' as and when they see fit, or more to the point, when a particularly good opportunity arises for them to make some 'easy money'. Those black young men as featured in this study who are involved in road culture may intermittently become embroiled within the world of 'badness', perhaps through their associations (friendly or antagonistic) with 'rude boys', however, such young men are neither committed to the values of the non conformist 'rude boys' nor to those of mainstream society. Extending Matza's (1964) concept of 'drift' beyond the theoretical confines of crime and deviance, it is possible to view the individual lifestyle and post-16 career choices made by my informants as being transient and sporadic. If it is possible to argue that the young black men are neither committed to 'badness' nor the values of mainstream society, then it might also follow that such young men (and their black female and white and mixed parentage peers) will also choose to judiciously dip in and out of full-time education and/or paid employment. Consequently, whilst accepting the macro constraints placed upon the young people as a result of social class, local 'place', race /ethnicity and gender, it can be argued that many of the lifestyle and post-16 career choices made by the young people have been largely motivated by 'drift' (Matza, 1964). The concept of 'drift' as used to explain the young people's individualised lifestyle and post-16 career choices does provide an alternative theoretical perspective. However, 'drift' perspective which emphasises the 'processes of individualisation may obscure the continuation of common routes and fates' (Ball et al., 2000: 145). Consequently, the impact of class and racial (discrimination) disadvantage upon the lives of the young people featured in this study should not be downplayed or underestimated.

It is clear that this study only provides a brief snapshot into the lives of those young people featured, their lifestyle and post-16 choices are not permanent or set in stone but will be subject to continual change. Many of the white young men have taken advantage of the current opportunities provided by the local economy and have secured full-time paid employment as labourers, forklift truck operators, and apprentice electricians. If I were to revisit Manor in five years time however, the local economy may have changed—whereby entry level employment routes into the building and construction industries may have disappeared—and equally the values and attitudes of the white young men to paid manual employment may also have changed. I might find on revisiting Manor that the members of the Grafters are long-term unemployed, or have decided to make a living 'ducking and diving' (Hobbs, 1998) within the underground economy. Similarly, members of the Arms House Crew who currently are working on road doing 'badness' may in the near future enter the labour market and/or take up opportunities within the education and training sectors. As youth researchers it is imperative that we caution against presenting young people as being 'more serious, more organised and planned than they really are' (Ball et al., 2004: 146).

At this point I must remind the reader that this study came about in part because of my own frustrations around the dearth of holistic and locally situated empirical research with regards black British youth. I have argued throughout this study that those discourses around the black youth (male) subject have tended to be viewed from a problematising (Pryce, 1979; Cashmore and Troyna, 1982; Sewell, 1997) or largely romanticised perspective (Hewitt, 1986; Jones 1991; Back, 1996). In the main the voices of young black British subjects have had very little opportunity to be heard on their own terms without first being re-interpreted by academics largely hamstrung by the theoretical biases inherent within contemporary cultural studies, the sociology of 'race relations' and 'ethnicity studies'. Within this study I have attempted to provide ample space and opportunities for the many competing and contradictory voices of my young informants to be heard. Hopefully, I have shown through my research that young people are neither soulless automatons who are helpless victims of the prevailing wider political and socio-economic conditions and structures. Equally, my young informants are not all rational individualists who plan their long-term futures (lifestyle, career and family-home life) and who live neat and 'risk managed' lives.

Whilst it would be easy for me to theorise and transpose my own academic biases upon the many voices of my young informants, I feel strongly feel that by doing so I would be defeating one of my research aims; to de-essentialise the black British young male subject. It is imperative that black British youth (like working-class white youth) are not lumped together and viewed as victims, social outlaws or sexy cultural innovators. There needs to be a great deal more holistic, locally situated empirical research undertaken with black (and other minority ethnic) young people—in large urban areas like London, Birmingham and Manchester and smaller localities such as High Wycombe, Burnley and West Bromwich—that explores the complexities and differences within contemporary black British youth experience(s). Such studies that are rooted within local neighbourhood settings would provide a greater body of evidence for youth researchers (like myself) to draw upon when arriving at their particular theoretical standpoint and final set of conclusions.

# Appendix

## The young people—informants and participants

*Tape recorded interviewees*

Little Man—male, African Caribbean, aged 13[1]
Mr Business—male, Indian, aged 15
Charley—female, white, aged 21
dj Wildstyle—male, African Caribbean, aged 21
Milly—female, Indian, aged 18
Maria—female, white, aged 17
Kandy—female, white, aged 18
Tony C—male, white, aged 18
Lazy Boy—male, (mixed parentage) white and black African, aged 20
Sweet Boy—male, African Caribbean, aged 17
Raymond—male, African Caribbean, aged 17
Martin—male, white, aged 15
Darlene—female, African Caribbean, aged 14
Kanya—female, African Caribbean, aged 14
Tall Boy—male, African Caribbean, aged 16
Eddie—male, African Caribbean, aged 19
Will—male, African Caribbean, aged 21
Melinda—female, white, aged 16
Ayesha—female, African Caribbean, aged 17
Griot—male, African Caribbean, aged 18
Tonya—female, African Caribbean, aged 16
Marcus—male, African Caribbean, aged 14

*Other participants*

*PUPS*

Simon Peters—male, (mixed parentage) white/white and black Caribbean, aged 15
Dwayne—male, (mixed parentage) white and black African, aged 15
Tee—male, African Caribbean, aged 15
Steven—male, African Caribbean, aged 14
Mikey—male, African Caribbean, aged 15
Big Boy—male, African Caribbean, aged 13
Che'—male, African Caribbean, aged 15
Nat—male, African, aged 13

1 Little Man's age (and all quoted ages of young people) at the time of interview, all other participants ages at start of field work.

Tye—male, (mixed parentage) white and black African, aged 14
Sen—male, African, aged 15
Tyler—male, African Caribbean, aged 13
Carl—male, white, aged 15

## Grafters

Sick Boy—male, white, aged 20
Sparky—male, white, aged 20
Stevie—male, white, aged 17

## Arms House Crew

Manley—male, African Caribbean, aged 18
Nathaniel—male, African Caribbean, aged 18
Louis—male, African Caribbean, aged 17
Nathaniel—male, African Caribbean, aged 18
Makki—male, Afican, aged 18
Redz—male, African Caribbean, aged 16
T Boy—male, African Caribbean, aged 17
Stylo—male, African Caribbean, aged 17
Gato—male, African Caribbean, aged 17
B-Line—male, African Caribbean, aged 16
Prince—male, African Caribbean, aged 24

## Others

Carol—female, African Caribbean, aged 16
Faye—female, (mixed parentage) white and black Caribbean, aged 15
Harry—male, African Caribbean, aged 24
Paul—male, (mixed parentage) black Caribbean and Indian, aged 17
David—male, African Caribbean, aged 21

# References

2001 Census, www.statistics.gov.uk/census2001/access_results.asp

Ackers, H. (1985), *Racism and political marginalisation in the metropolis: The relationship between black people and the Labour Party in London*, Unpublished Thesis: London University.

Ainley, P. (1994), *Degrees of difference: Higher education in the 1990s*, London: Lawrence and Wishart.

Alexander, C. (1996), *The art of being black: The creation of black British identities*, Oxford University Press.

Alexander, C. (2000), Black masculinity, in K. Owusu (eds), *Black British culture and society*, London: Routledge.

Ali Asghar, M. (1996), *The politics of community: Bangladeshi community organisations in East London*, London: Bangla Heritage Limited.

Allan, G. and Crow, G. (2001), *Families, households and society*, Basingstoke, Hants: Palgrave.

Amin, A. (1994), *Post-Fordism: A Reader*, Oxford: Blackwell.

Anderson, B. (1991), *Imagined communities: Reflections on the origin and spread of nationalism*, London: Verso.

Anderson, E. (1990), *Street wise: Race, class, and change in an urban community*, Chicago and London: The University of Chicago Press.

Anderson, E. (1999), *Code of the street: Decency, violence, and the moral life of the inner city*, New York; London: Norton 1999.

Armstrong, G. (1993), Like That Desmond Morris? in D. Hobbs, and T. May (eds), *Interpreting the field: Accounts of ethnography*, Oxford: Oxford University Press.

Ashford, S., Gray, J. and Tranmer, M. (1993), *The Introduction of GCSE exams and changes in post-16 participation*, Sheffield: Employment Department, Research and Development Series, Youth Cohort Series No.23.

Ashton, D., Maguire, M. and Spilsbury, M. (1990), *Restructuring the labour market: The implications for youth*. Basingstoke: Macmillan.

Auletta, K. (1982), *The underclass*, New York: Random House.

Aymer, C. and Okitikpi, T. (2001), *Young black men and the connexions service*, London: HMSO.

Back, L. (1996), *New ethnicities and urban multiculture: Racisms and multiculture in young lives*, London: UCL Press.

Back, L., Cohen, P. and Keith, M. (1999), *Finding the way home: Working Papers 2,3 and 4*, Centre for New Ethnicities Research, University of East London.

Ball, S., Maguire, M. and Macrae, S. (2000), *Choice, pathways, and transitions post-16: New youth, new economies in the global City*, London: Routledge/Falmer.

Banks, M., Breakwell, G., Bynner, J., Emler, N., Jamieson, L., and Roberts, K. (1992), *Careers and identities*, Milton Keynes: Open University Press.

Beck, U. (1992), *Risk society*, London: Sage.

Benn, N. (1999), *Dark Destroyer*, London: Blake.

Bermant, C. (1975), *Point of arrival*, London: Eyre Methuen.

Berthoud, R. (1999), *Young Caribbean men and the labour market*, York: Joseph Rowntree Foundation/ York Publishing Services.

Besant, W. (1901), *East London*, London: Charles and Windus.

Bhabha, H. (1994), *The location of culture*, London: Routledge.

Bidder, S. (2001), *Pump up the volume*, London: Channel 4 Books.

Blauner, R. and Wellman, D. (1973), Toward the de-colonization of social research, in J. Ladner. (eds), *The death of white sociology*, New York: Vintage.

Bloch, H. (1996), Refugees in Newham, in T. Butler, M. Rustin (eds), *Rising in the east: The regeneration of East London*, London: Lawrence and Wishart.

Blumer, H. (1969), *Symbolic interactionism*, New Jersey: Prentice-Hall.

Blundell, R., Griffith, R. and Windmijer, F. (1999), *Individual effects and dynamics in count data models*, London: Institute of Fiscal Studies.

Booth, C. (1889), *Labour and life of the people*, London: Williams and Northgate.

Booth, C. (1902), *Life and labour of the people* London: Macmillan.

Bourgois, P. (1995), *In search of respect: Selling crack in El Bario*, Cambridge: Cambridge University Press.

Bowling, B. (1998), *Violent racism: Victimization, policing and social context*, Oxford: Clarendon Press.

Bowling, B. and Phillips, C. (2002), *Racism, crime and justice*, Harlow: Longman.

Brannen, J., Dodd, K., Oakley, A., and Storey, P. (1994), *Young people, health and family life*, Buckingham: Open University Press.

Burgess, R. (1982), *Field research: A Sourcebook and Field Manual*, London: George Allen and Unwin.

Burney. (1990), *Putting street crime in its place: A report to the Community/Police Consultative Group for Lambeth*, London: Goldsmiths College.

Butler, T., Hamnett, C., Ramsden, M. and Mir, S. (2008) City to Sea: Some socio-demographic impacts of change in East London, in P. Cohen, and M. J. Rustin (eds), *London's turning: The making of Thames Gateway*, Aldershot: Ashgate

Cahill, C. (2000), Street literacy: Urban teenagers' strategies for negotiating their neighbourhood, *Journal of Youth Studies* 3:3. 251-277.

Callaghan, G. (1992), Locality and localism: The spatial orientation of young adults in Sunderland, *Youth and Policy* 39: 23-33.

Carrington, B. (1998), Sport, masculinity, and black cultural resistance, *Journal of Sport and Social Issues* 22:3. 275-298.

Cashmore, E. (1979), *Rastaman: The Rastafarian movement in England*, London: Allen and Unwin.

Cashmore, E. and Troyna, B. (1982), *Black youth in crisis*, London: George Allen and Unwin.

Chamberlain, M. (2001), Narratives of Caribbean families in Britain and the Caribbean, in H. Goulbourne, and M. Chamberlain (eds), *Caribbean families in Britain and the trans-Atlantic world*, London and Oxford: Macmillan Education.

Clark, G (1997) Regenerating East London: Where's the toolkit? *Rising East: The Journal of East London Studies* 1(2):55-74

Cohen, P. (1996), All white on the night/ Narratives of nativism on the Isle of Dogs, in T. Butler, and M. Rustin (eds), *Rising in the east; The Regeneration of East London*, London: Lawrence and Wishart.

Cohen, P. and Ainley, P. (2000), In the country of the blind?: Youth studies and cultural studies in Britain, *Journal of Youth Studies* 3(1): 79-95.

Cohen, S. (1955), *Delinquent boys: The culture of the gang*, Chicago: Chicago Free Press.

Cohen, S. (1972), *Folk devils and moral panics: The creation of mods and rockers*, London: MacGibbon and Kee.

Coles, Bob. (1995), *Youth and social policy: Youth citizenship and young careers*, London: UCL Press.

Coles, B., Hutton, S., Bradshaw, J., Craig, G., Godfrey, C., and Johnson, J. (2002), *Literature review of the costs of being 'Not in education, employment or training' at age 16-18*, DfES, London: HMSO.

Collier, R. (1998), *Masculinities, crime and criminology: Men, heterosexuality, and the criminal (ised) other*, London: SAGE Publications.

Connell, R. W. (1987), *Gender and power*, Cambridge: Polity Press.

Cornwell, J. (1984), *Hard earned lives: Accounts of health and illness from East London*, London; New York: Tavistock Publications: Methuen.

Corrigan, P. (1979), *Schooling the Smash Street Kids*, London: Macmillan.

Craine, S. (1997), The Black Magic Roundabout: Cyclical transitions, social exclusion and alternative careers, in R. McDonald (eds), *Youth, the underclass and social exclusion*, London: Routledge.

Crown Prosecution Service. (2003), *Race for justice: A review of Crown Prosecution Service decision making for possible racial bias at each stage of the prosecution process*, London: Crown Prosecution Service.

DCSF (2007) *Participation in education, training and employment by 16-18 year olds in England*, Statistical first release, www.dcsf.gov.uk/rsgateway/ DB/SFR/s000792/index. shtml [accessed 20 July 2008]

DCSF (2008a), *Participation in education, training and employment by 16-18 year olds in England*, www.dcsf.gov.uk/rsgateway/DB/SFR/s000792/index.shtml [accessed 20 July 2008]

DCSF (2008b), *Youth cohort study and longitudinal study of young people in England: The activities and experiences of 16 year olds: England 2007*, www.dcsf.gov.uk/rsgateway/ DB/SBU/b000795/index.shtml [accessed 20 July 2008]

Dennis, R. (1993), Participant observatrions, in J. H. Stanfield III and R.M. Dennis (eds), *Race and ethnicity in research methods*, London: Sage Publicatons.

Dench, G., Gavron, K. and Young, M. (2006), *The new East End: Kinship, race and conflict*, London: Profile Books

Donald, J. (1992), *Sentimental education: Schooling, popular culture and the regulation of liberty*, London: Verso.

Eade, J. (1989), *The Politics of community: The Bangladeshi community in East London*, Aldershot: Averbury.

Epstein, D., Elwood, J., Hey, V. and Maw, J. (1998), *Failing boys?, Issues in Gender and Achievement*, Buckingham: Open University Press.

Ericson, R. and Haggerty, D. (1999), Governing the young, in R. Smandych (eds), *Governable places: Readings on governmentality and crime control*, Aldershot: Ashgate.

Ermisch, J. and Francesconi, M. (2001), *The effects of parents' employment on children's lives*, London: Family Policies Studies Centre.

Evans, K., Fraser, P. and Watlake, S. (1996), Whom can you trust? The politics of 'grassing' on an inner city housing estate, *The Sociological Review* 44:3.

Faizi. (1986), *A history of the black presence in London*, London: The Greater London Council.

Featherstone, M. (1991), *Consumer culture and post modernism*, London: Sage.

Fetterman, D. (1998), *Ethnography: Step by step*, London: Sage Publications.

Ferrell, J., Hayward, K., Morrison, W. and Presdee, M. (2004), *Cultural criminology unleashed*, London: GlassHouse Press

Fielding, N. (1981), *The National Front*, London: Routledge and Kegan Paul.

Finch, J. and Mason, J. (1993), *Negotiating family responsibilities*, London: Routledge.

Fishman, W. (1979), *The Streets of East London*, London: Duckworth.

Fitzgerald, R., Finch, S. and Nove, A. (2000), *Black Caribbean young men's experiences of education and employment*, London: HMSO.

Fitzgerald, M., Stockdale, J. and Hale, C. (2003), *Young people and street crime*, London: Youth Justice Board for England and Wales.

Flood-Page, C., Campbell, S., Harrington, V., and Miller, J. (2000), *Youth crime: Findings from the 1998/99 youth lifestyles survey*, Home Office Research Study 209, London: Home Office.

Foster, J. (1990), *Villains*, London: Routledge.

Foster, J. (1999), *Docklands: Cultures in conflict, worlds in collision*, London: UCL Press.

Foucalt, M. (1977), *Discipline and punish*, London: Allen Lane.

Fryer, P. (1984), *Staying power: The history of black people in Britain*, London: Pluto Press.

Fuller, M. (1984), Black girls in a comprehensive school, in M. Hammersley, and P. Woods (eds), *Life in school: The sociology of pupil culture*, Milton Keynes: Open University Press.

Furlong, A. (1992), *Growing up in a classless society? School to Work Transitions*, Edinburgh: University of Edinburgh Press.

Furlong, A., Biggart, A., and Cartmel, F. (1996), Neighbourhoods, opportunity structures and occupational aspirations, *Sociology* 30(3): 551-566.

Furlong, A. and Cartmel, F. (1997), *Young people and social change: Individualization and risk in late modernity*, Buckingham: Open University Press.

Gans, H. (1982), The participant observer as human being: Observations on the personal aspects of fieldwork, in R. Burgess (eds), *Field research: A sourcebook and field manual*, London: George Allen and Unwin.

Garnham, N. (1998), Political economy and cultural studies: Reconciliation or divorce?, in J.Storey (eds), *Cultural theory and popular culture: A reader*, Hertfordshire: Prentice Hall.

Gelder, K. (1997), Introduction to part two, in K. Gelder, and S. Thornton (eds), *The subcultures reader*, London: Routledge.

Giddens, A. (1991), *Modernity and self identity: Self and society in the late modern age*, Cambridge: Polity Press.

Giddens, A. (1992), *The transformation of intimacy*, Cambridge: Polity.

Gillborn, D., and Gipps, C. (1996), *Recent research on the achievements of ethnic minority pupil: Report for the Office for Standards in Education*, London: HMSO.

Gillborn, D., and Mirza, H.S. (2000), *Educational inequality: Mapping race, class and gender—A synthesis of research evidence*, London: OFSTED.

Gilroy, P. (1982), Police and thieves, in Centre for Contemporary Cultural Studies, Birmingham University (eds), *The empire strikes back: Race and racism in 70s Britain*, London: Routledge.

Gilroy, P. (1987a), *There aint no black in the Union Jack: The cultural politics of race and nation*, London: Routledge.

Gilroy, P. (1987b), The myth of black criminality, in P. Scratton (eds), *Law, order and the authoritarian state*, Milton Keynes: Open University Press.

Gilroy, P. (1993a), *The black Atlantic: Modernity and double consciousness*, London: Verso.

Gilroy, P. (1993b), *Small acts: Thoughts and politics of black cultures*, London: Serpent's Tail.

Gordon, P. (1983), *White law: Racism in the police courts and prisons*, London: Pluto Press.

Goulbourne, H. (2001), The socio-political context of Caribbean families in the Atlantic world, in H. Goulbourne, and M. Chamberlain (eds), *Caribbean families in Britain and the trans-Atlantic world*, London: Macmillan Education.

Goulbourne, H. and Chamberlain, M. (2001), *Caribbean families in Britain and the trans-Atlantic world*, London and Oxford: Macmillan Education.

Gray, J., Jesson, D., and Tranmer, M. (1993), *England and Wales youth cohort study. boosting post-16 participation in full-time education: A study of some key factors*, Sheffield: Employment Department, Research and Development Series, Youth Cohort Series No.20.

Gray, O. (2003), Badness-honour, in A. Harriot (eds), *Understanding crime in Jamaica*, Kingston: University West Indies Press.

Griffin, C. (1997), Representations of the young, in J.Tucker, and S. Roche (eds), *Youth in society: Contemporary theory, policy and practice*, London: Sage Publications and Open University.

Griffiths, V. (1988), From 'playing out' to 'dossing out': Young women and leisure, in E.Wimbush, and M. Talbot (eds), *Relative freedoms: Women and leisure*, Milton Keynes: Open University.

Hall, S. (1991), Old and new identities, old and new ethnicities, in A.D. King (eds), *Culture globilization and the world system*, Hampshire: Macmillan.

Hall, S. (1992), New ethnicities, in J.Rattansi, and A. Donald (eds), *Race culture and difference*, London: Sage Publications and Open University.

Hall, S., Crichter, C., Jefferson, T., Clarke, J., and Roberts, B. (1978), *Policing the crisis: Mugging, the state and law and order*, London: Macmillan.

Hallsworth, S. (2005), *Street crime*, Devon: Willan.

Hammersley, M. (1992), *What's wrong with ethnography?* London: Routledge.

Hammersley, M. and Atkinson, P. (1983), *Ethnography: Principles in practice*, London: Tavistock Publications.

Harrington, V. and Mayhew, P. (2001), *Mobile phone theft*, Home Office Research Study 235, London: Home Office.

Hebdige, D. (1987), *Cut 'n' mix: culture, identity, and Caribbean music*, London: Comedia 1987.

Hesse, B. (1993), Black to front and black again, in M. Keith and S. Pile (eds), *Place and the politics of identity*, London: Routledge.

Hesse, B. and Dhanwant, K. (1992), *Beneath the surface: Racial harassment in the Borough of Waltham Forest*, Aldershot, Hants: Avesbury.

Hewitt, R. (1986), *White talk, black talk: Inter-racial friendship and communication amongst adolescents*, Cambridge: Cambridge University Press.

Hobbs, D. (1988), *Doing the business: Entrepreneurship, detectives and the working class in the East End of London*, Oxford: Oxford University Press.

Hobbs, D. and May, T. (1993), *Interpreting the field*, Oxford: Oxford University Press.

Hollands, R. (1990), *The long transition: Class, culture and youth training*, London: Macmillan.

Holme, A. (1985), *Housing and young families in East London*, London: Routledge and Kegan Paul.

Honigmann, J. (1982), Sampling in ethnographic fieldwork, in R.Burgess (eds), *Field research: A sourcebook and field manual*, London: George Allen and Unwin.

Hooks, B. (1991), *Yearning: Race, gender and cultural politics*, London: Turnaround.

Hooks, B. (1992), *Black looks: Race and representation*, Boston, MA: South End Press.

Hooks, B. (2004), *We real cool: Black men and masculinity*, New York and London: Routledge.

Husbands, C. (1979), 'The threat' hypothesis and racist voting in England and the United States, in R. Miles, and A. Phizacklea (eds), *Racism and political action in Britain*, London: Routledge and Kegan Paul.

Husbands, C. (1982), East End racism 1900-1980: Geographical continuities in vigilantist and extreme right-wing political behaviour, *London Journal* 8:1.

Husbands, C. (1983), *Racial exclusionism and the city: The urban support of the National Front*, London: Allen and Unwin 1983.

Husbands, C. (1994), Following the 'continental model'?: Implications of the recent electoral performance of the British National Party, *New Community* 20(4): 563-579.

Hutson, S. and Jenkins, R. (1987), *Taking the strain: Families, unemployment and the transition to adulthood*, Milton Keynes: Open University Press.

Jarvie, I. (1982), The problem of ethical integrity in participant observation, in R. Burgess (eds), *Field research: A Sourcebook and field manual*, London: George Allen and Unwin.

Jeffs, T. and Smith, M. (1987), *Youth work*, London: Macmillan Education.

Jeffs, T. and Smith, M. (1988), *Welfare and youth work practice*, London: Macmillan Education.

Johnston, L., Macdonald, R., Mason, P., Ridley, L. and Webster, C. (2000), *Snakes and ladders: Young people, transitions and social exclusion*, Bristol: Joseph Rowntree Foundation/Policy Press.

Jones, G. (1999), The Same People In The Same Places? Socio-Spatial Identities and Migration in Youth, *Sociology* 33(1): 1-22.

Jones, S. (1991), *White youth, black culture: The reggae tradition from JA to UK*, Basingstoke: Macmillan.

Katz, J. (1988), *Seductions of crime: Moral and sensual attractions in doing evil*, New York: Basic Books.

Keith, M. (1993), *Race, riots and policing*, London: UCL Press.

Keith, M. (1995), Making the street visible: Placing racial violence in context, *New Community* 21:4. 551-565.

Kiernan, K. (1992), The impact of family disruption in childhood on transitions made in young adult life, *Population Studies* 46: 213-234.

London Borough of Hackney. (2006), *Hackney Borough profile 2006*, Strategic Policy and Research Team, www.hackney.gov.uk/xp-hackney_borough_profile_2006.pdf [accessed 20 November 2008].

London Borough of Newham. (1999), *Economic background information*, Unitary Development Plan, Department of Environment and Planning.

London Borough of Newham. (2007), *Focus on Newham 2007: Local people and local conditions*, Corporate Research Unit, www.newham.gov.uk/NR/rdonlyres/56801C30-C760-4E9B-9607-4E3D94B73C70/0/FON_Key_Stats_2007.pdf [accessed 20/10/2008]

Lash, S. and Urry, J. (1994), *Economies of signs and space*, London: Sage.

Lawrence, E. (1982), In abundance of water the fool is thirsty: Sociology and black pathology, in Centre for Contemporary Cultural Studies, Birmingham University (eds), *The Empire strikes back: Race and racism in 70s Britain*, London: Routledge.

Lea, J., and Young, J. (1984), *What is to be done about law and order?* Harmondsworth: Penguin.

Lieber, M. (1976), 'Liming' and other concerns: The style of street embedments in Port-Of-Spain, Trinidad, *Urban Anthropology* 5(4): 319-333.

Liebow, E. (1967), *Tally's corner: A study of negro street-corner men*, Boston, MA:: Little Brown and Co.

Lloyd, T. (1999), *Young men, the job market and gendered work*, York: Joseph Rowntree Foundation/ York Publishing Services.

Mac an Ghail, M. (1988), *Young gifted and black: Student-teacher relations in the schooling of black youth*, Milton Keynes: Open University Press.

MacDonald, R. (1994), Fiddly jobs, undeclared working and the 'something for nothing society", *Work, Employment and Society* 8: 507-30.

MacDonald, R. (1997), Dangerous youth and the underclass, in R, MacDonald. (eds), *Youth, the 'underclass' and social exclusion*, London: Routledge.

MacDonald, R., Mason, P., Shildrick, T., Webster, C., Johnston, L. and Ridley, L. (2001), *Snakes and ladders: In defence of youth transition*, Sociological Research Online, 5(4): www.socresonline.org.uk/5/4/macdonald.html.

MacDonald, R. and Marsh, J. (2005), *Disconnected youth? Growing up in Britain's poor neighbourhoods*, London: Palgrave

MacDonald, R., and Shildrick, T. (2007), Street Corner Society: Leisure careers, youth (sub)culture and social exclusion, *Leisure Studies*, 26(3): 339-355

MacLeod, J. (1987), *Ain't no makin' it: Aspirations and attainment in a low-income neighbourhood*, Oxford: Westview Press.

Maguire, M. and Maguire, S. (1997), Young people and the labour market, in R, MacDonald. (eds), *Youth, the 'underclass' and social exclusion*, London: Routledge.

Majors, R. (1989), Cool pose: The proud signature of black survival, in M.S. Kimmel, and M.A. Messener (eds), *Men's lives*, New York, NY: Macmillan.

Majors, R. (1990), Cool pose: Black masculinity and sports, in M.A. Messner and D.F. Sabo (eds), *Sports, men and the gender order: Critical Feminist Perspectives*, Champaign, IL: Human Kinetics.

Majors, R., Wilkinson, V., Gulam, B. (2000), Mentoring black males in Manchester: Responding to the crisis in education and social alienation, in Owusu, K. (eds), *Black Culture and society*, London: Routledge.

Majors, R. and Billson, J.M. (1992), *Cool pose: The dilemnas of black men in America*, New York, NY: Lexington Books.

Malbon, B. (1998), The club: Clubbing, consumption, identity and the spatial practices of every-night life, in T. Skelton. G. Valentine (eds), *Cool places: Geographies of youth cultures*, London: Routledge.

Mann, W. (2008), One hundred and twenty years of regeneration, from East London to the Thames Gateway: Fluctuations of housing type and city form, in P. Cohen, and M. J. Rustin (eds), *London's turning: The making of Thames Gateway*, Aldershot: Ashgate

Marriot, D. (1996), Reading black masculinities, in M. Mac an Ghail (eds), *Understanding masculinities: Social relations and cultural arenas*, Buckingham: Open University Press.

Matza, D. (1964), *Delinquency and drift*, New York: Wiley.

Matza, D. (1969), *Becoming deviant*, New Jersey: Prentice-Hall.

May, J. (1996), Globilization and the politics of place: Place and Identity in an inner London neighbourhood, *Royal Geographical Society* 21:194-215.

Mayer, M. (1994), Post-Fordist politics, in A, Amin (eds), *Post Fordism: A reader*, Oxford: Blackwell.

McCarthy-Brown, K. (2001), *Mama Lola: A vodou priestess in Brooklyn*, London: University of California Press.

McDowell, L. (2001), 'Its that Linda again': Ethical, practical and political issues involved in longitudinal research with young men, *Ethics, Place and Environment* 4:2. 87-100.

McDowell, L. (2004) *Redundant Masculinities? Employment Change and White Working Class Youth*, Blackwell, Oxford.

McGuigan, J. (1992), *Cultural populism*, London: Routledge.

McNamee, S. (1998), 'The home': Youth, gender and video games: Power and control in the home, in T. Skelton, G.Valentine (eds), *Cool places: Geographies of youth cultures*, London: Routledge.

McVicar, D. and Rice, P. (2001), *Participation in further education in England and Wales: An analysis off post war trends*, Oxford Economics Papers, www.soton. ac.uk/~econweb/dp

Meadows, P. (2001), *Young men on the margins: An overview report*, York: Joseph Rowntree Foundation/ York Publishing Services.

Mercer, K. (1993), Just looking for trouble: Robert Mapplethorpe and fantasies of race, in A. McGuigan, and J. Gray (eds), *Studying culture: An introductory reader*, London: Edward Arnold.

Mercer, K., and Julien, I. (1988), Race, sexual politics and black masculinity: A Dossier, in Rutherford, R. Chapman and J. (eds), *Male order: Unwrapping sexuality*, London: Lawrence and Wishart.

Mirza, H.S. (1992), *Young, female and black*, London: Routledge.

Muncie, J. (2004), *Youth and crime: A critical introduction*, London: Sage.

Mungham, G. (1982), Workless youth as a moral panic, in T. Rees, and P. Atkinson (eds), *Youth, unemployment and state intervention*, London: Routledge and Kegan Paul.

Mumford, K. and Power, A. (2003), *East Enders: Family life and community in East London*, Bristol: Policy Press

Murdock, G. (1993), Cultural studies at the cross roads in A. McGuigan, A. J. Gray (eds), *Studying culture: An introductory reader*, London: Edward Arnold.

Murray, C. (1984), *Losing ground*, New York: Basic Books.

Murray, C. (1990), *The emerging British underclass*, London: Institute of Economic Affairs.

Nayak, A. (2003), *Race, place and globalization: Youth cultures in a changing world*, Oxford: Berg

Newham.com (2008) *Refugees and asylum: Welcoming refugees and asylum seekers into our communities*, 2012games.newham.gov.uk/About+Newham/NewhamsCommunities/New+to+Newham-Refugees.htm [accessed 20/10/2008]

NMP/CARF. (1991), *Newham Monitoring Project/ Campaign Against Racism and Fascism. Newham: The Forging of a Black Community.* London: Newham Monitoring Project.

O' Brien, M., and Jones, D. (1996), Family Life in Barking and Dagenham, in T. Butler and M. Rustin. (eds), *Rising in the East: The Regeneration of East London,* London: Lawrence and Wishart.

ODPM (2004), *Index of Multiple Deprivation,* London: Office for the Deputy Prime Minister

ONS (2006) *East London Employee Jobs Data 2006,* Office for National Statistics Population Survey, www.nomisweb.co.uk |accessed 13/10/2008|

Panayi, P. (1993) *Racial Violence in Britain 1840-1950,* Leicester: Leicester University Press.

Parker, H. (1974), *View From The Boys,* London: David and Charles.

Parry, O. (1996), Unmasking Masculinities in the Caribbean Classroom, *Sociological Research Online* 1.

Patrick, J. (1973), *A Glasgow Gang Observed,* London: Eyre Methuen.

Patterson, S. (1965), *Dark Strangers: A Study of West Indians in London,* Middx: Pelican.

Pearce, J. (1996), Urban Youth Cultures: Gender and Spatial Forms, *Youth and Policy* 52: 1-11.

Pearson, G. (1983), *Hooligan: A History of Respectable Fears,* London: Macmillan.

Pennant, C. (2002), *CASS,* London: John Blake Publishing.

Phillips, M. and Phillips, T. (1998), *Windrush: The Irresistible Rise of Multi-Racial Britain,* London: Harper Collins.

Polley, M. (1998), *A History of Sport and Society Since 1945,* London: Routledge.

Porter, R. (1994), *London: A Social History,* Harmondsworth: Penguin.

Poynter, G. (1996), Manufacturing in East London, in T. Butler, and M. Rustin (eds), *Rising in the East: The Regeneration of East London,* London: Lawrence and Wishart.

Pryce, K. (1979), *Endless Pressure,* London: Bristol Classical Press.

Reay, D. and Lucey, H. (2000), I Don't Really Like It Here But I Don't Want To Be Anywhere Else: Children and Inner City Council Estates *Antipode* 32(4): 410-428.

Redhead, S. (1990), *The End of the Century Party: Youth and Pop Towards 2000,* Manchester: Manchester University Press.

Redhead, S. (1993), *Rave off: Politics and Deviance in Contemporary Youth Culture,* Aldershot: Avebury.

Reynolds, S. (1998), *Energy Flash: A Journey Through Rave Music and Dance Culture,* London: Picador.

Reynolds, T. (2001), Caribbean Fathers in Family Lives in Britain, in H. Goulbourne, and M. Chamberlain (eds), *Caribbean Families in Britain and the Trans-Atlantic World,* London and Oxford: Macmillan Education.

Reynolds, T. (2005), *Caribbean Mothers: Identity and Experience in the U.K,* London: Tufnell Press

Riemer, J. (1977), Varieties of Opportunistic Research, *Urban Life* 5(4): 467-77.

Riley, R. and Young, G. (2000), *New Deal for Young People: Implications for Employment and Public Finances Research and Development,* Research and Development Report ESR62, Sheffield: Employment Service.

Rix, V. (1996), Social and Demographic Change in East London, in T. Butler, and M. Rustin (eds), *Rising in the East: The Regeneration of East London,* London: Lawrence and Wishart.

Rix, V. (1997), Industrial Decline, Economic Restructuring and Social Exclusion in London East, 1980s and 1990s, *Rising East: The Journal of East London Studies* 1:1. 118-141.

Roberts, K. (1993), Career trajectories and the mirage of increased social mobility, in I. Bates, and G. Riseborough (eds), *Youth and inequality,* Buckingham: Open University Press.

Roberts, K. (1997), Is there an emerging British underclass?, in R.MacDonald, (eds), *Youth, the 'underclass' and social exclusion,* London: Routledge.

Robinson, C. (2000), Creating space, creating self: Street-frequenting youth in the city and suburbs, *Journal of Youth Studies* 3(4): 429-443.

Roche, J and Tucker, S. (1997), *Youth in society: Contemporary theory, policy and practice,* London: Sage Publications and Open University.

Rose, N. (1993), Government, authority and expertise in advanced liberalism, *Economy and Society* 22: 283-299.

Rose, N. and Miller, P. (1992), Governing the enterprising self, in P. Heelas, and P. Morris (eds), *The values of the enterprise culture: The moral debate,* London: Routledge.

Roseneil, S. (1993), Greenham revisited: Researching myself and my sisters, in D. Hobbs, and T. May (eds), *Interpreting the field,* Oxford: Oxford University Press.

Rustin, M. (1996), Perspectives on East London: An introduction, in T. Butler, and M. Rustin (eds), *Rising in the east; The regeneration of East London,* London: Lawrence and Wishart.

Rustin, M. (1997), What can a journal contribute to East London regeneration? *Rising East: The Journal of East London Studies* 1(2): 15-31.

Sanders, B. (2005), *Youth crime and youth culture in the inner city,* London: Routledge.

Sansone, L. (2003), *Blackness without ethnicity: Constructing race in Brazil.* Basingstoke: Palgrave MacMillan

Saunders, N. (1995), *Ecstacy and the dance culture,* London: Neal's Yard Press.

Scheurich, J. (1997), *Research method in the postmodern,* London: Falmer.

Sewell, T. (1997), *Black masculinities and schooling: How Black Boys Survive Modern Schooling,* Staffordshire: Trentham.

Shildrick, T. (2006), Youth culture, subculture and the importance of neighbourhood, *Young,* 14(1):61-74

Sivanandan, A. (1982), *A different hunger: Writings on black resistance,* London: Pluto Press.

Smith, M. (1988), *Developing youth work: Informal education, mutual aid and popular practice,* Milton Keynes: Open University Press.

Smith, R.T. (2001), Caribbean families: Questions for research and implications for policy, in H. Goulbourne and M. Chamberlain (eds), *Caribbean families in Britain and the trans-Atlantic world.* London and Oxford: Macmillan Education.

Smith, J. (2003), *The nature of personal robbery,* London: Home Office Research Study 254.

Social Exclusion Unit. (1998), *Truancy and school exclusion,* London: HMSO.

Social Exclusion Unit. (1999), *Bridging the gap: New opportunities for 16-18 year olds not in education, employment or training,* Social Exclusion Unit, London: HMSO.

Solomos, J. (1988), *Black Youth Racism and the State,* Cambridge: Cambridge University Press.

Stanfield, J.H. (1993), Epistemological considerations, in J.H. Stanfield III, and R.M. Dennis (eds), *Race and ethnicity in research methods*, London: Sage Publications.

Stanko, A. and Newburn, T. (1994), *Just boys doing business?: Men, masculinities and crime*, London: Routledge.

Staples, R. (1982), *Black masculinity: The black man's role in American society*, San Francisco, CA: Black Scholar Press.

Stenson, K. and Factor, F. (1995), Governing youth: New directions for the youth service, in J. Baldock, and M. May (eds), *The Social Policy Review no. 7*, Canterbury: Social Policy Association.

Stenson, K. (1998), Beyond histories of the present, *Economy and Society*, 27(4):333-352.

Stenson, K. (1999), Crime, control, governmentality and sovereignty, in R. Smandych. (eds), *Governable places: Readings on governmentality and crime control*, Aldershot: Ashgate.

Stenson, K. (2000), Crime control, social policy and liberalism, in G. Lewis, S. Gerwirtz, and J. Clarke (eds), *Rethinking social policy*, London: Sage.

Stockdale, J. and Gresham, P. (1998), *Tackling street robbery: A comparative evaluation of operation Eagle Eye*, Police Research Group Crime Prevention Unit Series Paper 36, London: Home Office.

Stolzoff, N. (2000), *Wake the town and tell the people: Dancehall culture in Jamaica*, Durham and London: Duke University Press.

Sullivan, M. L. (1989), *'Getting paid': Youth crime and work in the inner city*, Ithaca: Cornell University Press.

Taylor, I. (1981), *Law and order: Arguments for socialism*, London: Macmillan.

Taylor, I., Evans, K. and Fraser, P. (1996), *A tale of two cities: A study in Manchester and Sheffield*, London: Routledge.

Thornton, S. (1995), *Club cultures: Music, media and subcultural capital*, Cambridge: Polity.

Tizard, B., and Phoenix, A. (1993), *Black, white or mixed race; Race and racism in the lives of young people of mixed parentage*, London: Routledge.

Van Deburg, W.L. (2004), *Hoodlums: Black villains and social bandits in American life*, London: University of Chicago Press.

Waddington, P.A.J., Stenson, K. and Don, D. (2004), In proportion: Race, and police stop and search, *British Journal of Criminology* 44: 889-914.

Wallace, C. (1987), *For richer for poorer: Growing up in and out of work*, London: Tavistock.

Waters, M. (1995), *Globalization*, London: Routledge.

Watt, P. (1998), Going out of town: Race, and place in the South East of England, *Environment and Planning D: Society and Space* 16: 687-703.

Watt, P., and Stenson, K. (1998), The street: It's a bit dodgy around there: Safety, danger, ethnicity and young people's use of public space, in T. Skelton, and G. Valentine (eds), *Cool places: Geographies of youth cultures*, London: Routledge.

Watt, P. (2003), Urban marginality and labour market restructuring: Local authority tennants and employment in an inner London Borough, *Urban Studies*, 40(9): 1769-1789.

Webster, C. (1996), Local heroes: Violent racism, localism and spacism among Asian and white young people, *Youth and Policy* 53: 15-27.

Westwood, S. (1990), Racism, black masculinity and the politics of space, in J. Hearn, and D. Morgan (eds), *Men, masculinities and social theory*, London: Unwin Hyman.

White, J. (1980), *Rothschild buildings: Life in an east end tenement block*, London: Routledge and Kegan Paul.

Williams, T., and Kornblum, W. (1985), *Growing up poor*, Lexington, MA: Lexington Books.

Williamson, H. (1993), Youth policy in the United Kingdom and the marginalisation of young people, *Youth and Policy* 40: 33-48.

Williamson, H. (1997), Status zero youth and the 'underclass': Some considerations, in R. MacDonald (eds), *Youth, the 'underclass' and social exclusion*, London: Routledge.

Willis, P. (1977), *Learning to labour: How working class kids get working class jobs*, Farnborough: Gower.

Wilmott, P. (1966), *Adolescent boys of East London*, Harmondsworth: Pelican Books Limited.

Wright, C. (1985), School process—An ethnographic study, in S. Eggleston, D. Dunn, and M. Anjali (eds), *Education for some: The educational and vocational experiences of 15-18 year old members of minority ethnic group*, Stoke-on-Trent: Trentham.

Wright, R., Brookman, F. and Bennett, T. (2006), The foreground dynamics of street robbery in Britain, *British Journal of Criminology* 46(1): 1.

Wulff, H. (1995), Inter-racial friendship: Consuming youth styles, ethnicity and teenage femininity in South London, in V. Wulff, and H. Amit-Talai (eds), *Youth Cultures: A Cross Cultural Perspective*, London: Routledge.

Young, J. (1986), The failure of criminology: The need for a radical realism, in J. Young, and R. Mathews (eds), *Confronting crime*, London: Sage.

Young, M., and Wilmott, P. (1957), *Family and kinship in East London*, Harmondsworth: Penguin Books Limited.

Young, J. (2003), Merton with energy, Katz with structure: The sociology of vindictiveness and the criminology of transgression, *Theoretical Criminology* 7:3.

Lightning Source UK Ltd.
Milton Keynes UK
UKOW04f0022040914

237999UK00001B/34/P